Beach to Bluegrass

Places to Brake
on Virginia's Longest Road

Joe Tennis

The Overmountain Press

JOHNSON CITY, TENNESSEE

For my son, John Patrick

ISBN-10: 1-57072-323-0
ISBN-13: 978-1-57072-323-0
Copyright © 2007 by Joe Tennis
Printed in the United States of America
All Rights Reserved

2 3 4 5 6 7 8 9 0

Letter From the Author

My father came up with the main title of this book, *Beach to Bluegrass,* when I told him I wanted to write about US-58, the longest road in Virginia. This title refers to US-58's ramble across Virginia's southern border, linking the sandy shores of the Atlantic Ocean to Cumberland Gap National Historical Park at the Bluegrass State of Kentucky. Yet the "bluegrass" also has a musical meaning across Virginia's Blue Ridge Mountains, as more than 100 miles of US-58 have been designated the "Crooked Road," a bluegrass music trail connecting Mabry Mill and Galax to my adopted hometown of Bristol.

I was born off US-58 at Virginia Beach. My wife and daughter were also born along this route. But for them, the journey began along the Tennessee-Virginia border, some 400 miles away. While I was writing this book, my son, John Patrick, almost arrived on US-58 at Bristol as I raced my wife to the hospital.

I have spent most of my life along this diverse route. As a kid, I rowed a boat on the Elizabeth River in Norfolk. As an adult, I've paddled the New River in Grayson County. I've climbed both Mount Rogers and Mount Trashmore. I've watched the sunset over Buggs Island Lake and the sunrise over the Blue Ridge. I've written numerous articles about the people in Clarksville, Chesapeake, Hiltons, Hillsville, Duffield, Damascus and places in between.

Beach to Bluegrass shares the stories of these great places—from Clinchport to Portsmouth—and the people who live in them. With a mix of history and legend, the tales of this trail relate and intertwine with each other, all tied together by that long and winding road.

Joe Tennis
Bristol, Virginia

Contents

Acknowledgments

Special thanks for help in this project to Daniel Rodgers, Carlos Wilson, Harold Barkley, Mike West, Steven West, Col. William J. Davis, Albert Joynes, Deloras Freeman, Robin K. Rountree, Lee King, Connie Henderson, Dave Sadowski, David and Eileen Sadowski, Cara Ellen Modisett, Frank Malone, Jack Hite, Elaine Bowers, Scott Shanklin, Julian Hudson, Mary Page Richardson, Linda Williams, Robert Benning, Ed and Carol Brown, James Shepperd, Debbie Connolly, Wyatt Barczak, Julie Allen, Roger Reynolds, Ellen Brown, John Reynolds, Tim Cable, Tom Perry, John Grooms, Henry Ayers, Ella Sue Joyce, Sharoll Shumate, Coy Lee Yeatts, Ann Vaughn, Ronald W. Hall, Nancy Riggins, Paul Dellinger, Shirley Gordon, Bob McKinney, Jan Patrick, David and Nerine Thomas, Jaye and Joan Baldwin, Jack and Rubinette Niemann, Henny Schuster, Skip Blackburn, Lawrence Dye, Pete Sheffey, Bill McKee, Donnamarie Emmert, Mary Dudley Porterfield, Richard Rose, Debbie Addison, Jennifer Estep, Eleanor Walker Jones, Robert Weisfeld, William Booker, V. N. "Bud" Phillips, Tim Buchanan, Steve and Kim Rhodes, Sean Hyler, Darlene Cole, Rita Forrester, Fern Carter Salyer, Tim White, Rex and Lisa McCarty, Teresa Harless, Braven Beaty, Bob and Suzy Harrison, Frank Kilgore, Lucille Cowden Necessary, Craig Seaver, Tony Scales, Jerry Cox, Judy Davidson, Rebecca Jones, Robert Estes, Rhonda Robertson, Billy Heck, Donnie Harris, Carl Mullins, Carol Borneman, Scott Teodorski, Steve Galyean, the staff of the Washington County Public Library in Abingdon, and the Overmountain Press.

Sincere appreciation also to family members Maggie Caudill; James and Melissa Caudill; Rob and Michelle Tennis; Pat and Angie Wolfe; Dr. Walter Wolfe; my parents, Richard and Jeanette Tennis; my wife, Mary; and most especially my daughter, Abigail, for traveling the highways and constantly cheering "58!" and "Beach to Bluegrass!"

Preface

In the early days of the American colonies, going beyond the Appalachian Mountains to the bluegrass of Kentucky would be like when the Jamestown settlers sailed the Atlantic Ocean to reach the beach of Virginia. The journey to either destination was filled with mystery and confrontation.

Beach to Bluegrass links these journeys with its own across Virginia, from Cape Henry to the Cumberland Gap, serving tales of triumph and tragedy sandwiched between the "Gateway to the New World" and the "Gateway to the West."

The 58-chapter story lies largely along US-58, Virginia's longest road. This east-to-west highway spans more than 500 miles and passes through every type of town and terrain imaginable in the Old Dominion, from the traffic-tied Hampton Roads to the pastoral piedmont, the lofty Blue Ridge to the once-perilous Powell Valley, lying as far west as Detroit.

US-58 ranges from ten lanes in urban Virginia Beach to two-lane sprints that are as serpentine as streams. Large parts of the highway follow the Crooked Road, Virginia's heritage music trail, as well as Daniel Boone's Wilderness Road.

The journey of *Beach to Bluegrass* connects manmade and natural landmarks, meeting famous generals and musicians, a witch, a waterfall, a schoolhouse in a cyclone, and a lake that never was. Collectively, these passages tell many great stories of Virginia, and much about America.

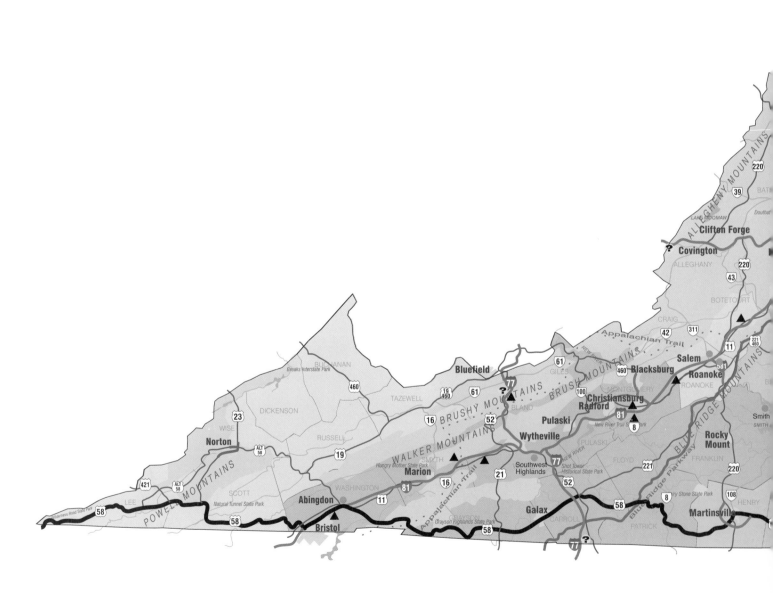

Hampton Roads

Water and war define Hampton Roads, a region rich in military landmarks, legends, and lore. Also called "Tidewater," it's an area webbed with a network of urban rivers dotted by birds, boats, and the crab-pot buoys of working watermen.

The name "Hampton Roads," historically, refers not to land but the shipping lanes in the rivers surrounding several cities. Virginia's longest road cuts through the heart of this scene, slipping past downtown districts both old and new while reaching ever westward across a series of swamps.

Beach

For five days and nights, storms raged over the ocean. Waves crashed, lightning flashed, rain pounded. And there! In the middle of all that mess stood Virginia, just as morning broke on April 26, 1607.

A tired band of more than 100 Englishmen feasted hungry eyes. And, probably, they dreamed of gold. Their three ships—*Discovery, Susan Constant,* and *Godspeed*—had traveled across the Atlantic Ocean for more than four months, first casting off in England before Christmas of 1606. Their plan to land in Virginia, for the Virginia Company of London, must have seemed like a modern-day mission to the moon.

These men had orders to launch the first permanent, English-speaking colony in the New World. But they must have been wary, knowing that equally ambitious Spanish explorers could be waiting to attack. And, less than a generation earlier, other Englishmen had tried the same idea on nearby Roanoke Island, North Carolina, and had simply vanished.

These men of 1607 had fights. Capt. John Smith, a war veteran, got shackled in one of the ship's prisons for an alleged mutiny.

These men had superstitions. Master George Percy kept a journal of the expedition and noted "a blazing Starre" on February 12. That comet was seen as a sign of impending doom.

These men, also, had greed. Many believed Virginia held a wealth of gold, and they were willing to brave the Atlantic Ocean to find it, even though

Chesapeake Bay at First Landing State Park

Beach at Cape Henry, inside Fort Story, with breakwaters built to prevent erosion

people thought sea serpents might wander out of the waves, or beasts could be lurking in the jungles of this mysterious, virgin land.

Making landfall, the crew explored what are now the sandy shores of Cape Henry in Virginia Beach, Virginia, at the mouth of the Chesapeake Bay. They discovered a paradise Percy described as "faire meddowes and goodly tall Trees, with such Fresh-waters running through the woods." But, that same day, the English were ambushed. Percy wrote, "the Savages creeping on all foure, from the Hills like Beares, with their Bowes in their mouthes, charged us very desperately in the faces."

These "Savages" of the sand "Hills" wounded two men, Capt. Gabriel Archer and Mathew Morton, a sailor. Obviously, these Chesapeake Indians viewed the foreigners as a threat. For years, the Indians had lived in this coastal area. And now here comes these overdressed, odd-speaking, fanciful strangers who acted like they owned the place.

Original Cape Henry Lighthouse, built in 1791–1792

The English later explored the Chesapeake Bay in a small boat called a "shallop." They also marched on land, finding more fires, more oysters, and what Percy called a "good store of Mussels." Finally, giving thanks to God for their safe journey, the men spent April 29 erecting a wooden cross at Cape Henry, a place they named for the Prince of Wales and son of King James I.

Then they left. Capt. Christopher Newport, in following orders of the Virginia Company, rejected settling at Cape Henry, fearing the cape was too exposed in case of attack. So the men sailed up the James River. On May 13 they reached a swampy isle they called Jamestown. There, the English established the long-suffering village that grew into the foundation of America.

No one knows exactly where the English landed at Cape Henry. Some say the first landing occurred south of the cape at what is now Virginia Beach's 49th Street, the site of a sealed-up inlet once leading to Crystal Lake. Others guess the landing might have been westward, just inside the Chesapeake Bay toward the Lynnhaven River.

Geographically, Cape Henry juts out of Virginia Beach with the odd shape of a duck head. The bill points west to the mouth of the Lynnhaven, and the head curves along the Chesapeake Bay until it reaches the Atlantic Ocean. At the center lies the Desert, which is marked by a maritime forest, tall pines, and 100-foot-high sand dunes, possibly what Percy called "the Mountaines." For more than two centuries after the English arrived, the Desert remained in the public domain at Cape Henry's "Gateway to the New World."

Cape Henry, though, was dark and dangerous. At

The English fired a musket, and the Indians, according to Percy, "retired into the Woods with a great noise and so left us."

The following day, the English walked a few miles inland and found a fire where the natives had been roasting oysters. The Indians were gone, having "fled away to the Mountaines," Percy noted, so the explorers "ate some of the Oysters, which were very large and delicate in taste."

New Cape Henry Lighthouse

First Landing Cross

times, it was illuminated with big bonfires. But pirates would play games with the flames by moving those fires, confusing sailors, and then plundering ships.

In 1789, the newly formed United States Congress approved lighting up the sky. Two years later, New York's John McComb, Jr., began building an octagonal lighthouse at Cape Henry atop a 40-foot-high sand dune. Fish oil was used to fuel the lighthouse lamps, but that oil soaked into the wooden staircase and continually posed a fire hazard.

The sandstone lighthouse never succumbed to fire. Instead, cracks on the foundation put the landmark out of commission. In 1881, the lighthouse was left standing as a second Cape Henry Lighthouse was built just 357 feet away. This new beacon, rising 163 feet, or about twice the height of the first, was made of black-and-white cast iron.

Around the two lighthouses, a collection of cottages grew at Cape Henry. And those oysters! Those same juicy Lynnhaven oysters that Percy's group had stolen from the Indians—and relished with such delight—would be making history again.

President William Howard Taft ate so many Lynnhaven oysters at Cape Henry in 1909 that he said he felt "like an oyster." The fat and happy president then proposed building a fortress at Cape Henry—what became Fort Story, an army base named for Gen. John P. Story. This base grew into one of the most heavily fortified areas on the Atlantic coast by World War II, taking on such nicknames as "Gibraltar of the East."

Much of Cape Henry's nearby Desert became Virginia Beach's Seashore State Park in 1936, later renamed First Landing State Park. The preserve includes sand "Hills" and "Mountaines" plus cypress pools of "Fresh-waters," marshy "faire meddowes," and "goodly tall Trees."

Nearby, a stone cross was planted inside Fort Story in 1935 to replicate the wooden cross the English had erected centuries earlier. The landmark was dedicated on April 26, commemorating that stormy day in 1607 when the English set foot on that mysterious, virgin land.

🚗 *Virginia Beach: Cape Henry & First Landing State Park*

Cape Henry lies inside the Fort Story Military Reservation in Virginia Beach. To get there, follow US-60 (Atlantic Ave.) for four miles north of Laskin Road (US-58/31st St.). Beyond the entrance gate, continue north for one mile to the Cape Henry lighthouses and the First Landing Cross. To reach First Landing State Park from the Fort Story gate at the junction of 89th Street and Atlantic Avenue, continue west on US-60 (Shore Dr.) for 3.5 miles. The 2,888-acre park includes a campground, hiking trails, a playground, and a visitor center.

Monopoly on the Oceanfront

Talk about a "Monopoly" on the oceanfront. Streets in the resort area of Virginia Beach share names not only with Atlantic City, New Jersey, but these same avenues—Atlantic, Pacific, Mediterranean, and Baltic—show up on the board game Monopoly. In Virginia Beach, you can even sleep in a hotel on Boardwalk!

Originally, the Virginia Beach Boardwalk was made of actual boards in 1888, not cast in concrete like it is today. It also flanked the fabulous Princess Anne Hotel, a landmark that faced the Atlantic Ocean and catered to famous folks like President Grover Cleveland and Alexander Graham Bell. The Princess Anne Hotel featured a ballroom, a post office, and enough space for 400 people.

But, just before daybreak on June 10, 1907, the hotel caught fire, forcing guests to escape in their pajamas. Suddenly, the finest hotel on the Virginia Beach shoreline was gone. That same fire consumed much of the original five-block boardwalk.

Virginia Beach stayed little more than a colony of cottages dotting the dunes for the next few years. But then, in 1927, the private Laskin Road became a public highway leading to the three-block-long Seaside Park Casino, and a new Virginia Beach Boardwalk was paved along the sand.

Still, this little Atlantic City needed more, something grand for dignitaries, something like the old Princess Anne Hotel. In April 1927, the Town of Virginia Beach got all that with the celebrated opening of a real-life castle called the Cavalier.

Talk about a monopoly on the oceanfront. The Cavalier had it. There wasn't anything in Virginia Beach like it. The looming landmark stood seven stories, composed of more than 500,000 bricks and surrounded by 60 acres of manicured grounds. It was the town's tallest building and designed like a Y-shaped pillar of Colonial architecture. The Cavalier could fill the void left by the destruction of the Princess Anne Hotel. But, unlike the Princess Anne, the Cavalier did not sit down at the Boardwalk—it stood far above, perched on a sand dune.

When the $2,000,000 hotel opened as part of "a scheme for the building up of Virginia Beach as a health and recreational resort," Norfolk's *Virginian-Pilot* called the enterprise a "Great Resort Development at [the] Gateway of New World."

Inside, the Cavalier lobby offered a barbershop, a

The Cavalier Hotel in Virginia Beach

his death, which occurred during Prohibition, remain a mystery. Stories cannot say whether the founder of the Adolph Coors Company was pushed or fell on his own. Either way, a legend whispered among the walls of the Cavalier says that the ghost of Adolph Coors can now be seen as an unexplained image of a man that shows up in photographs.

Longtime doorman Carlos Wilson could not say much about Coors. That event took place before his time, even though Wilson began working at the Cavalier in 1938 at age 15. Still, while on the job at age 84, Wilson recalled his own ghostly encounter in a kitchen near the Hunt Room of the Cavalier.

"I heard some pans rattling on my way upstairs, and I was checking out that night," Wilson said. "I saw a shadow behind the cooking range. I got on close to it. And it just vanished and went away."

Wilson started to leave, but he heard the pans rattling again. He turned. "I went back to make sure that I wasn't seeing things," he said. "And as soon as I got close to it, it just vanished and went away."

At first, Wilson told no one about seeing the shadow or hearing the rattles, until a fellow employee volunteered a corroborating story. After that, Wilson said, "I knew it was a ghost."

The Cavalier, itself, looked ghostly during the blackouts of World War II. The Navy used the hotel for three years as a radar training school, and classes

beauty parlor, a dress shop, a drugstore, and a stockbroker's office. Also, in bedrooms, guests could lap up luxury with taps running four kinds of water—hot, cold, ice-cold, and salt water for bathing.

The hotel, nicknamed the "Aristocrat of the Virginia Seashore," hosted the likes of writer F. Scott Fitzgerald, actress Judy Garland, and artist Hank Ketchum, who showed up in 1953 and featured the Cavalier in his "Dennis the Menace" cartoon sketches. Several presidents booked accommodations. And the one who resigned, President Richard Nixon, stayed overnight and had fireside chats with fellow guests in the Hunt Room, a private men's club for hunters, horsemen, and fishermen.

There was also Adolph Coors, the man whose name is on canned and bottled beer. At age 82, Coors fell from a window on the sixth story of the Cavalier on June 5, 1929. But the circumstances of were sometimes moved to the dark bottom of the indoor swimming pool.

At the end of the war, lights shined all night as people celebrated at the Cavalier Beach Club, a ritzy room that once hosted big bands led by the likes of Benny Goodman and Guy Lombardo.

In 1973, it looked like the party was over for the Cavalier. The then-outdated hotel was shuttered, as a more modern hotel—the Cavalier Oceanfront—opened a bit closer to the beach. The original hotel reopened in 1976 and was later renovated, but it was a long, slow ascent for the Cavalier to regain its former glory.

Now standing as a symbol of pre-Depression prosperity, the Cavalier overlooks Virginia Beach's dozens of newer, more modern hotels with a well-deserved attitude. That would include, even, looking down at its younger sibling, the Cavalier Oceanfront, lodged beside the original, near the ocean's edge.

Towering hotels and the Atlantic Ocean border the Virginia Beach Boardwalk.

🚗 *Virginia Beach: The Cavalier Hotel & the Boardwalk*

From the junction of 89th Street and US-60 (Atlantic Ave.) near Fort Story, follow VA-60 south for four miles to Laskin Road (US-58/31st St.). At the terminus of Laskin Road, a 26-foot-tall King Neptune statue stands along the Virginia Beach Boardwalk, close to the junction of Laskin Road and Atlantic Avenue; the Seaside Park Casino formerly stood nearby. To find the Cavalier Hotel from here, go one block west on Laskin Road to Pacific Avenue, then go north for a half mile. The 1927 hotel is on the left; the 1973 structure stands on the right at 42nd Street and Pacific. From Laskin Road, Atlantic Avenue stretches 14 blocks south to meet the terminus of US-58 Business (17th St./Virginia Beach Blvd.). Here, a bronzed statue of muscle man John Wareing overlooks the ocean at the Boardwalk. The late Wareing owned a Virginia Beach gym; he became famous for televised stunts, like holding back a motorcycle with his teeth. The Wareing statue stands about a block north of the site of the Princess Anne Hotel, which stood in the vicinity of 16th Street.

Note: Virginia Beach's Old Coast Guard Station stands at 24th Street and Atlantic Avenue, about halfway between the two routes of US-58. The station features exhibits on the maritime history of Virginia Beach.

Rejoice for Rose Hall

Virginia Beach grew from a tiny town into the "World's Largest Resort City" after merging with Princess Anne County in 1963. Land values also skyrocketed, especially along Virginia Beach Boulevard, where almost every block seems blitzed with commercial development. Almost every block, spare the seven acres that surround the Francis Land House. Curiously, this brick landmark stands like an island in the city's asphalt sea, and no one knows when it was built. But "1732" is mysteriously etched into a brick in the cellar, and that was once used to date the structure.

The Francis Land House originally belonged to a prosperous family that just could not get enough of using the same name for each successive generation. It's believed that five or maybe six men named Francis Land lived here, as early as the 1650s, on what was once a 1,020-acre plantation in now-extinct Princess Anne County. Possibly, the Land family built this house around 1805 or 1810, according to a scientific analysis of the brickwork, hand-hewn timbers, and the floor's pine planks. Behind the house, small boats could once navigate the narrow Pine Tree Branch, a silted-in stem of the Lynnhaven River.

The Francis Land House, or Rose Hall

In 1853, the Georgian style house passed out of the Land family. One century and one year later, it passed into the hands of Colin Studds, who extensively remodeled the house for Rose Hall Dress Shop for the Ladies and Their Daughters. But then Rose Hall was sold, and the upscale dress shop was fitted for a wrecking ball. In fact, it was so sure to be destroyed that a photo caption in a pictorial book lists the landmark as "scheduled to be torn down in 1974 to make way for a new shopping center."

Still, there would be rejoicing for Rose Hall. In 1975, the house remained intact, and the Virginia Beach City Council voted on buying it. Half the council said yes. The opposing half said paying $735,000 for the house and the surrounding 35 acres was "extremely expensive" and a case of "excessive spending." Stepping into the fight, Mayor J. Curtis Payne cast the deciding vote, and 11 years later, the Francis Land House opened as a city-owned museum, interpreting the long-lost lifestyle of old Princess Anne County.

🚗 *Virginia Beach: Francis Land House*

From Atlantic Avenue, both US-58 Business (17th St./Virginia Beach Blvd.) and Laskin Road (US58-/31st St.) span about four miles, going west, until joining near Great Neck Road (VA-279). The US-58 Business route slips through the residential community of Seatack (named for its proximity to a "sea attack" on Cape Henry during the War of 1812), while the parallel path of Laskin Road climbs over Hilltop (named for a 27-foot-high hill on the crest of Pungo Ridge). West of Great Neck Road, the combined US-58 runs 1.5 miles to the Francis Land House, on the left, at 3131 Virginia Beach Blvd. The house is listed on historic landmark registers.

Make a Mountain out of a Landfill

When Virginia Beach built a grassy mountain, it got as trashy as it could get. The city piled up old motors, tires, refrigerators, food scraps, and newspapers, all before the days of recycling. All through the early 1970s, it stacked up 640,000 tons of trash.

The idea came from Roland E. Dorer, the director of the state's Bureau of Solid Waste and Vector Control. Dorer figured it was better to pile trash rather than dig down and disturb the city's shallow groundwater supply.

So, with layer after layer of garbage and dirt, the city covered all of its rotting debris. It would make a mountain out of a landfill. Then, comically dubbing the hill "Mount Trashmore," the old garbage dump became a major city park.

At a height of 68 feet, Mount Trashmore registers as barely a blip on a topographic map. But still, this gently sloping peak could compete with Cape Henry's sand dunes for being the tallest elevation on the Virginia Beach flatlands.

At the side of the mountain lies the city seal, a round emblem displaying symbols of Virginia Beach history, like the first Cape Henry lighthouse. One legend said the huge seal could be opened and that trash could still be put inside the mountain. That's not true. Then, neither was the story about Mount Trashmore's impending explosion of "low-flying dirt clods" in 1992.

That year, on April Fool's Day, morning deejays on rock radio station WNOR-FM broadcast that Mount Trashmore was in big trouble. They said a seismologist had inspected this old landfill and that a high amount of methane gas was building up, and—oh, golly—Mount Trashmore was just about to blow!

Morning commuters must have laughed. The stunt was, after all, an April Fool's Day joke. It was all just rubbish. But something went awry as deejays Henry Del Toro and Tommy Griffiths announced evacuation routes. Their broadcast sounded too real. Many people panicked, calling the city's parks and recreation office. Others clogged the emergency phone lines.

The Federal Communications Commission later investigated the incident and sent the station's owners a letter of admonition. The joke about the former landfill also turned into a stinky situation for the station's staff, with some members tied up on suspension without pay for as long as two weeks.

Mount Trashmore, a former city dump turned city park

🚗 *Virginia Beach: Mount Trashmore Park*

From the Francis Land House, follow US-58 (Virginia Beach Blvd.) for three miles west to Virginia Beach's downtown district at Pembroke (named for a nearby brick home called "Pembroke," built in 1764). To reach Mount Trashmore, turn left on Independence Boulevard and go 1.4 miles. Then turn left on Edwin Drive to enter Mount Trashmore Park. The mountain can be climbed using concrete steps. The park includes a playground, fishing lakes, and picnic areas. From here, retrace the route to US-58 at Independence Boulevard.

Witch in an Eggshell

Grace Sherwood got whopped with charges of being a witch and was literally tied up, a true case of sink or swim. Later, the legends of her life grew like the rosemary that she had allegedly smuggled home from England in an eggshell.

Consider the time, not long after the witch-hunt scares of Salem, Massachusetts, in 1692. What's now called Virginia Beach was then called Princess Anne County, named for Anne, the daughter of King James II of England. Folks in this close-knit and proper society knew of the witchery that had spellbound Massachusetts, and they must have feared that some of that madness was spreading to their seaside farms, especially where Grace Sherwood lived in the Pungo area along Muddy Creek.

Either that, or Grace Sherwood just couldn't get along with others.

In the late 1690s, neighbors accused Sherwood of blighting their cotton crops, bewitching the weather, and causing cows to give sour milk. The uproar caused Sherwood and her husband, James, to boil over like cauldrons, and they slammed back with a series of slander suits.

In particular, Grace Sherwood went hex-to-head with Elizabeth Barnes, a woman who had accused her of coming into her room late one night and riding her. Barnes also said that Sherwood turned herself into a black cat and slipped out of her room through either a keyhole or a crack in the door.

More gossip grew around an odd story saying Sherwood was a witch in an eggshell. Folks said that Sherwood could make herself so small that she could fit inside an eggshell, and that she used it to scramble across the Atlantic Ocean to England. Returning in a single night, Sherwood brought back a batch of rosemary that, according to legend, has been growing wild ever since.

Unfortunately for the Sherwoods, all the slander suits did little but cast a spell on them. They couldn't win their cases. And, when James Sherwood died in 1701, Grace was left a widow with three sons and even more vulnerable for attack.

The feisty widow did win a case against Mr. and Mrs. Luke Hill after Mrs. Hill had physically beaten Sherwood. But that trial's outcome seemed to antagonize the Hills, who fought back by formally accusing Sherwood of witchcraft in court. Sherwood, subsequently, was strip-searched by an all-female jury,

A Virginia Beach neighborhood takes its name from the story of Grace Sherwood.

which declared that she had weird-as-witch markings on her body.

Next, the court of Princess Anne County ordered a trial by water, and Sherwood consented to an odd but simple test. Her right big toe was tied to her left thumb, and her left big toe was tied to her right thumb. Sherwood would be tossed into water, a substance that was believed to deem people good or evil. If she sank, she would be innocent but, obviously, dead. If she didn't sink, she was clearly a witch.

The day of the trial arrived. On July 10, 1706, folks flocked to the ducking by the hundreds. They cried "Duck the witch!" along the shore of the Lynnhaven River and treated the event as a circus.

Sherwood proved that she had the trappings of a circus-quality performer. In an act that even Harry Houdini would have admired, she managed to untie herself and float to the surface of the river. But, of course, look at what that proved—she was allegedly capable of witchcraft. Fished out of the water, she was cast into the county jail.

Little is known about Sherwood beyond her jail time, or exactly how long she stayed locked up. Royal Gov. Alexander Spotswood granted Sherwood several acres of land in 1714. She died in 1740.

Even with death, her legend persists. It's said that in her last breaths, Sherwood asked one of her sons to put her feet at her fireplace's warm ashes. The next day, Sherwood was not only dead, but gone, and all that remained in the ashes was a hoofprint.

Sherwood's story never died. The celebrated tale of her "witch duck" has lent its name in Virginia Beach to a point of land, a road, a housing subdivision, a shopping center, and a bingo parlor. The ducking was reenacted in 2003, with actors playfully gathering along the Lynnhaven River. Kayakers cried "Duck the witch!" Twin sisters Gale Johnson and Molly McDermott took turns playing Sherwood. Three years later, on the 300th anniversary of the trial, Gov. Tim Kaine formally exonerated Sherwood, declaring her no longer a witch.

🚗 *Virginia Beach: Witch Duck Point*

From Independence Boulevard, follow US-58 west for 1.1 miles to Witchduck Road at an intersection called "Chinese Corner" (named for a Chinese man who farmed here circa 1900). Turn right on Witchduck Road and follow for 1.7 miles. Turn left on Sullivan Boulevard and go about 200 yards, then turn right on North Witchduck Road and proceed for 1.5 miles (crossing Independence Blvd.). Pass into the Witch Duck Point neighborhood. This area marks the vicinity where the 1706 ducking of Grace Sherwood took place. The Witch Duck Bay, part of

This statue of Grace Sherwood stands on the corner of North Witchduck Road and Independence Boulevard.

the Lynnhaven River, is not publicly accessible here by land, but some of the river can be seen between houses along the road, which intersects the appropriately named "Sherwood Lane" and "Witch Duck Bay Court." A life-size statue of Sherwood stands in a grass median, near a historic marker, at the intersection of North Witchduck Road and Independence Boulevard. From this point, retrace the route to US-58.

Chimneytown

In the middle of World War I, a rash of random fires broke apart businesses in downtown Norfolk. Firemen fought flames alongside the city's soldiers, sailors, and marines on January 1, 1918. But water froze on clothing, icicles hung on hair, and one fireman was killed when he was caught beneath burning timbers at the old Monticello Hotel. Estimated property loss: $2,000,000.

Norfolk's famous cannonball, a gift from Lord Dunmore

During another war, after another fiery New Year's Day, you would have had a hard time even finding Norfolk.

Lord Dunmore sparked that story. This last royal governor of Virginia fled the Colonial capital at Williamsburg in 1775. Dunmore sent men to Norfolk to destroy a newspaper known for criticizing him. Then he took control of the press and printed his own paper, declaring martial law and offering freedom for slaves who took up arms. That same year, Dunmore's troops skirmished with patriot soldiers at Kempsville in what is now Virginia Beach and Great Bridge in present-day Chesapeake.

But Dunmore really took aim at Norfolk, a port town with about 6,000 residents. His small squadron of ships sat at Norfolk's harbor on the Elizabeth River while patriot soldiers teased British sailors from shore, even sticking their hats on bayonets and waving, like a dare. Finally, in gridlock, Dunmore's fleet opened fire and blasted cannons on January 1, 1776.

Homes and businesses flew into flames. And Dunmore's men landed on shore, torching Norfolk's warehouse row. Colonial rebels, meanwhile, ran in gangs and burned buildings that belonged to Dunmore's loyalists.

Truth be told, colonists burned most of Norfolk. But Dunmore got the blame in newspapers. The following February, Colonial troops burned whatever was left to deprive Dunmore of shelter. Then, with hardly more than chimneys popping out of rubble, "Norfolk Towne" became "Chimneytown" for the rest of the Revolutionary War.

Today, little more than the brick walls of St. Paul's Episcopal Church predate Norfolk's fires of 1776. It took a decade to rebuild the church. But something was missing; a cannonball, long lodged in the church's south wall, had fallen from its perch. In 1848, a servant digging with a spade discovered the ball about two feet below the earth. Symbolically, the weapon—now a famous reminder of the "Chimneytown" era—

was patched in place above an immortal inscription: FIRED BY LORD DUNMORE / JAN. 1, 1776.

🚗 *Norfolk: St. Paul's Episcopal Church*

From the Witchduck Road intersection, follow US-58 west into Norfolk for seven miles, passing Military Circle Mall and Broad Creek, in a commercial district. On the right, at 1010 Church St., stands the 1919 Attucks Theatre, the oldest theater in the nation that was designed, developed, financed, and operated entirely by African-Americans. Three blocks west of the theater, turn left on Monticello Avenue and veer left as the road immediately turns into St. Paul's Boulevard. The UFO-shaped building standing on the right is Norfolk Scope, a civic center. A half mile beyond Norfolk Scope, St. Paul's Episcopal Church stands at the corner of St. Paul's Boulevard and City Hall Avenue. Dating to 1739, the church is listed on historic landmark registers and is open to visitors.

The Old Soldier Sailed Away

The Old Soldier Sailed Away

Gen. Douglas MacArthur talked about going to war with "Red" China. But as a 13-year-old newspaper boy in Norfolk, he had trouble hawking what's black, white, and read all over.

Young Douglas was afraid to make newspaper sales, facing competitors his age. Once, even, he returned to his mother's family home with an unsold stack of newspapers. There, his mother simply told him to be a good salesman, no matter what.

The next day, MacArthur sold every newspaper. But this time he returned with ripped clothes, a black eye, a bloody face, and torn-up knuckles.

MacArthur remained a fighter—a Romanesque warrior, you might say. He became a five-star general and spent a 52-year career in the Army, serving in several wars. Then, at the end of his 84 years, it looked like the old soldier sailed away, with his final resting spot in a Navy town, Norfolk, where his body lies encased in marble beneath a two-story rotunda.

The general's parents had married at Norfolk in 1875. But his mother's family, the Hardys, hardly warmed to MacArthur's father, a Union Army officer. Some of the Hardy men, after all, had fought for the Confederacy during the Civil War.

In 1880, Douglas MacArthur was born at Little Rock Barracks, Arkansas, four years after the birth

The MacArthur Memorial in downtown Norfolk

of his oldest brother, Arthur MacArthur III. Another MacArthur boy—Malcolm, in the middle—died in childhood and was buried in 1883 at Norfolk.

In 1951, the general visited the site of his mother's Norfolk home, the now-demolished Riveredge, standing along the Elizabeth River. By then, his beloved mother had long been laid to rest at Arlington National Cemetery. A decade later, MacArthur would make plans for his own memorial in Norfolk.

As an officer in the Army and the son of an officer, MacArthur really had no home. He had lived all over the world. Still, Norfolk held a connection to the Hardys. Long-lost brother Malcolm was buried there. And, besides, Norfolk had offered its 1850 City Hall to be the MacArthur Memorial, with a museum and repository plus a gift shop selling replicas of the general's famous corncob pipe.

MacArthur's body arrived in 1964, after 3,000 people turned out for his funeral in Norfolk at St. Paul's Episcopal Church. By the turn of the next century, the boy who had scuffled on Norfolk's streets would also have his name on another landmark: a three-level urban shopping center called the MacArthur Center.

Norfolk: MacArthur Memorial

From St. Paul's Episcopal Church, continue one block west on City Hall Avenue to the MacArthur Memorial, on the left, at the corner of Bank Street. MacArthur Center stands between the church and the memorial. The memorial building is listed on historic landmark registers and features a library of MacArthur's papers plus exhibits on his life. A theater, also, shows a film documenting the general's career. The museum is open for tours and contains the tombs of Douglas MacArthur and his second wife, Jean.

Oh, Elizabeth

She slips in and out by the tug of the moon. And she curls around cities with floating tugboats, battleships, and barges.

Oh, Elizabeth! Capt. John Smith sailed between this river's sandy shores in 1608. Going about six or seven miles inland with a crew, Smith observed tall pines, cultivated fields, and Native American lodges.

Oh, how Smith would be lost today. The Elizabeth

Legend says that you once could walk from Norfolk to Portsmouth on the bows of boats in the busy harbor of the Elizabeth River.

has since been dredged to twice its original depth. It has lost up to two-thirds of its original width. And about half of its wetlands have been filled or drained since World War II, destroying the habitats of oysters, crabs, birds, and fish.

First called Chesapeake after the local Indians, the river was renamed for Princess Elizabeth Stuart, daughter of King James I of England. Really, though, it's not a river; the Elizabeth is actually a tidal arm of the lower Chesapeake Bay.

President George Washington authorized the construction of Fort Norfolk along the river in 1794, and the fort stayed busy through the War of 1812. But by 1848, Fort Norfolk had simply become the home of a squatter, Lemuel Fentress, who not only moved in but also billed the War Department $1,500, saying he had taken care of the place.

Confederates later used Fort Norfolk during the Civil War to supply ammunition to the CSS *Virginia*, one of the world's first iron ships. The hulking ironclad was built in Portsmouth on top of an old wooden boat called the *Merrimack*.

In 1862, the *Virginia* stormed down the Elizabeth, shooting apart the Union's wooden ships and instantly obsoleting the wooden navies of the world. That March, the *Virginia* confronted a Union ironclad, the USS *Monitor,* where the Elizabeth meets the James River at Hampton Roads. This meeting marked the world's first battle of iron ships. But the confrontation was a draw; neither ship could really damage the other. In the next few weeks, however, the Union took over both Norfolk and Portsmouth. Fearing then that the *Virginia* would be captured, the Confederates blew up their iron ship at Craney Island, near the mouth of the Elizabeth River.

🚗 Norfolk/Portsmouth: Elizabeth River

From the MacArthur Memorial, follow City Hall Avenue west for one block. Turn left on Atlantic Street and go three blocks to the Waterside, a shopping center overlooking the Elizabeth River with a dock for passenger ferries connecting Norfolk's Town Point Park to Portsmouth's Olde Towne. To the right, on One Waterside Drive, stands Nauticus, the National Maritime Center, which features extensive nautical exhibits. From the Waterside, go two blocks east on Waterside Drive. Turn left on St. Paul's Boulevard, and go one mile to rejoin US-58. Turn left and pass both the Harrison Opera House and the Chrysler Museum of Art, on the right, within 0.3 miles. US-58 then becomes Duke Street, and the route turns right on Brambleton Avenue.

Immediately cross Smith Creek at Ghent (an 1890s-era neighborhood named for the Treaty of Ghent, which ended the War of 1812). To find Fort Norfolk, continue a half mile beyond the Smith Creek bridge, turn left at Colley Avenue, go 0.3 miles, and turn right on Front Street. The fort is operated by the Army Corps of Engineers and is not always open to the public. Retrace the route from Fort Norfolk to the Colley Avenue intersection at Brambleton Avenue. Continue west on US-58 for 0.7 miles to enter the mile-long Midtown Tunnel to Portsmouth beneath the Elizabeth River.

The Commodore

*I*t should have been smooth sailing for James Barron. The Navy man had been promoted to the rank of Commodore. And, at 39, he commanded his own ship, the *Chesapeake*.

But soon after setting sail for the Mediterranean on June 22, 1807, the British frigate *Leopard* stopped Barron's ship off the coast of Virginia, and a messenger said four deserters were aboard the *Chesapeake*. Barron refused to allow the British to search the *Chesapeake*. In return, the *Leopard* opened fire, blasting Barron's boat at a distance of less than 200 feet.

The *Chesapeake* was helpless. It wasn't properly fitted for battle, and much of the crew was inexperienced or sick. Finally, for the sake of honor, Barron fired one shot and then ordered his flag lowered. By then, three men had been killed and at least 18 were wounded.

The British boarded Barron's surrendered ship and carted off the alleged deserters. The badly wounded Barron sailed the *Chesapeake* back to Norfolk.

Americans were outraged. Why, it all sounded incredulous. To be fired on in peacetime! Within days, President Thomas Jefferson ordered all armed vessels of Great Britain to leave the territorial waters of the United States. And then? The public, and especially officers of the Navy, hunted a scapegoat. Their scorn fell on Barron.

In 1808, Commodore Barron was put on court-martial. He tried to explain that the *Chesapeake* had

Commodore James Barron's grave

The Commodore Theatre in Portsmouth

been under repair, that the cannons were unmounted, that the ship was defenseless. His arguments were to no avail. Barron was kicked out of the Navy for five years without pay and found guilty of "neglecting, on the probability of an engagement, to clear his ship for action."

Ultimately, tensions between the United States and Great Britain flared into the War of 1812. Separately, too, Barron and the *Chesapeake* sailed into even more doom. The British captured the *Chesapeake* off the coast of Massachusetts. Barron's job on a merchant ship, meanwhile, left him marooned in Denmark and unable to safely cross the Atlantic Ocean until the end of the war.

All the while, Commodore Stephen Decatur publicly criticized Barron, especially for the *Chesapeake-Leopard* affair. Again, Barron tried to explain the particulars of the encounter, again to no avail. Finally, for the sake of honor, Barron challenged Decatur to a duel.

On March 22, 1820, the two commodores met on a field at Bladensburg, Maryland, just outside Washington, D.C. Each man fired one shot at eight paces. Barron was struck near the groin and fell to the ground, crying, "Decatur, I forgive you from the bottom of my heart." Almost as soon, Decatur exclaimed, "Oh, Lord, I am a dead man!"

Decatur dropped on the ground and simply lay there. He made peace with Barron but died later that night.

It took more than a year for Barron to heal from his gunshot wound, and even more time for the public to forgive him for killing Decatur, a popular prince among Navy officers. Yet, once again, Barron would try to explain himself, this time at a trial of his Navy peers in 1821. But not every mark was cleared against him, and it was still a few more years before Barron was assigned a new post in the Navy.

In some circles, Barron's name was never cleared. As an old man, he was recognized as a leading citizen of Norfolk and a senior officer in the Navy. He over- saw Portsmouth's Gosport Navy Yard for six years. And he was still called the Commodore when he died in 1851. Yet some could not resist adding, "He was the one who killed Decatur."

A century later, Barron was honored. His title, the Commodore, showed up in lights when a Portsmouth movie theater was named for him in 1945. Curiously, the theater marquee nearly illuminates Barron's grave, nearby, on the lawn of the Trinity Episcopal Church.

🚗 *Portsmouth: Commodore Theatre & Trinity Episcopal Church*

Coming out of the Midtown Tunnel on the Portsmouth side, continue west on US-58 for 1.7 miles. Turn left on High Street and go 1.4 miles to the Commodore Theatre, 421 High St. Commodore James Barron's grave lies inside a wrought-iron fence at the lawn of Trinity Episcopal Church, next to the Commodore Theatre, at the corner of Court and High streets. Both the church and the theater are listed on historic landmark registers.

Iron Fist and Sticky Fingers

Hardly anyone admired the style of Union Maj. Gen. Benjamin Butler, especially the people of Portsmouth and Norfolk during the Civil War. This cross-eyed, middle-aged lawyer from Massachusetts ruled these occupied cities with an iron fist and sticky fingers.

Particularly, Butler had a fetish for knives, forks, and spoons. He inspected houses and earned his nickname "Spoons" for pocketing people's silverware.

Butler won another tag—"The Beast"—for doing much worse. He seized funds set aside for children in Norfolk orphaned by the yellow fever plague of 1855. He charged oystermen a monthly fee to tong the rivers and bays. He levied a tax on all goods shipped into his military district. Butler also made a rule that every fourth dog would be killed unless the owner paid a two-dollar ransom.

At Portsmouth's Olde Towne neighborhood, Butler made his headquarters at the William Peters House, a Colonial Revival structure built in 1859. Butler's soldiers moved into other private homes, and they became infamous for stealing or destroying property while conducting inspections.

Beginning May 10, 1862, Union troops occupied Portsmouth for three years. During that time, a home at the corner of Crawford and London streets became

William Peters House in Olde Towne Portsmouth, built in 1859

known as the "Pass House" because citizens would have to obtain a pass there in order to leave town. Federal soldiers might also make Portsmouth's people take an oath of allegiance to the Union.

One old woman said no. Then, when faced with not obtaining a pass or even going to jail, the woman finally agreed. Without hesitation, she exclaimed, "Damn every Yankee soldier to hell!"

After that, the woman asked God's forgiveness for swearing and said, "While I was taking an oath, I thought I might as well make it strong."

🚗 *Portsmouth: Olde Towne*

From High Street at Trinity Episcopal Church, turn left on Court Street at Four Corners (site of the large Confederate War Memorial, constructed in 1881). Go 0.4 miles through Olde Towne to the privately owned William Peters House, 315 Court St., on the right. The Olde Towne Historic District spans about 20 blocks and includes Colonial, Federal, Greek Revival, Georgian, and Victorian architectural styles. Continue straight for two blocks past the Peters House to Crawford Parkway and an overlook of Crawford Bay on the Elizabeth River. Turn right and follow for a half mile as the road becomes Crawford Street. Turn right on High Street and return two blocks to Four Corners, where the 1846 Courthouse, 420 High St., houses a museum with local history exhibits. From here, continue following High Street for two miles to US-58 (Airline Blvd.).

Glorious Paradise

William Drummond escaped the quicksand, the briars, and the bobcats. He had journeyed to the center of the Great Dismal Swamp in 1665 and found a mysterious pool with waters the color of whiskey. That lake was later named for Drummond. Yet no one knew why Drummond was the only hunter in his group to survive that trip through these weird wetlands.

Maybe that's not surprising. The Great Dismal Swamp can be deadly. The forest teems with rattlesnakes. And it's a given you'll get religion if you get lost beneath its thick summertime canopy. You may never find your way out of the endless log ferns, inky puddles, and prickly thorn bushes.

Still, this is not half the swamp it used to be. The Dismal once spread across 500,000 acres. But it was logged from the late 1700s to as late as 1976 and has lost up to half its size. What remains on the Virginia–North Carolina border covers about 110,000 acres in the Great Dismal Swamp National Wildlife Refuge.

The swamp smells both sweet and pungent. It looks both rich and desolate. It sounds both lonely and crowded with the calls of warblers, hawks, and heron.

The name "Dismal Swamp" may sound gloomy, but it's actually quite repetitive. The words *dismal* and *swamp* were once interchangeable. Over time, this place became both.

William Byrd II hated it. In 1728, this aristocratic Englishman sloshed through the swamp—and nearly got killed—while surveying the boundary between Virginia and North Carolina. Byrd called the Dismal a "vast body of mire and nastiness" and a place where "foul damps ascend without ceasing, corrupt the air, and render it unfit for respiration."

However, Byrd saw opportunity. He suggested the Dismal be drained and used for farms. George Washington would later agree. In 1763, a young Washington rode his horse around the entire swamp, surveying the ground. Washington also dropped his surveying equipment, according to legend, and hopped on a juniper tree to escape a bear.

By George, the swamp began to change. The Father of Our Country called the Dismal a "glorious paradise" and figured it would be a good spot to grow rice. Only, it really wasn't. The peat soil hardened like cement.

Still, Washington remained adventurous. He rounded up a group of influential partners, including

Dismal Town Boardwalk in the Great Dismal Swamp

mal Town." But, in years to come, some slaves became so familiar with the area that they ran away and used the swamp as a refuge from their dismal lives.

Both Washington and Virginia Gov. Patrick Henry proposed plans to build a canal through the swamp. Construction began in 1793, and the shallow Dismal Swamp Canal was completed in 1805, tying the Southern Branch of the Elizabeth River to the Pasquotank River at Elizabeth City, North Carolina. Boats used the canal to reach the long-gone Lake Drummond Hotel, which straddled the state line. Some came here for quick weddings, since North Carolina allowed marriages at a young age. Others came to fight duels, since you could simply run to the next state to avoid punishment.

Many, too, drank the whiskey-colored water of Lake Drummond. The roots and bark of juniper and cypress trees have turned this lake water brown. Even so, sailors once favored this "juniper water" on long voyages, since it can stay fresh for up to a year.

Lake Drummond is one of only two natural fresh-water lakes in Virginia. The other, Mountain Lake, lies near a fault line in Giles County and is known for draining and refilling itself through rock crevices that shift during earthquakes. One tremor in 1959 caused crystal-clear Mountain Lake to rise by 20 feet. A drought in 2001 nearly made the 100-foot-deep Mountain Lake disappear.

Controlled by a dam operated by the Army Corps of Engineers, much larger Lake Drummond's levels don't fluctuate like those at Mountain Lake. The sandy-bottom lake lies on an elevation higher than most of the surrounding swampland. And it's no small pond. At 3,100 acres, Lake Drummond spans more

Dr. Thomas Walker, an explorer famous for finding the Cumberland Gap in search of Kentucky's blue-grass. By the late 1760s, Washington's partners owned 40,000 acres of swampland. They called their operations "Dismal Swamp Land Company" and "Adventurers for Draining the Great Dismal Swamp." These men slashed up the swamp with artificial waterways, such as the nearly five-mile-long Washington Ditch, used to transport timber. Each partner contributed money plus five slaves to the effort.

A few slaves lived in shacks at a place called "Dis-

Lake Drummond in the Great Dismal Swamp

than 55 times the size of the 55-acre Mountain Lake. However, it reaches depths of only about six feet.

How was Lake Drummond formed? Possibly, it's a collapsed sinkhole. Or, maybe, a slow fire burned a hole in the swampy peat, and that filled with water. Maybe there's some truth to the Native American legend about a giant "fire bird" above the swamp; per-

haps this oval-shaped lake was formed by a meteor crash.

Hosts of other legends surround the swamp, from sightings of a "swamp creature" that allegedly looks like Bigfoot to the famous Lady of the Lake paddling her white canoe on Lake Drummond. People have seen this lady, her lover, and her lamp, which is reputedly powered by fireflies. Or, at least, they think they have. Mysterious lights that hover above the lake surface have also been attributed to fox fire, an illumination produced by certain fungi as wood decays.

Still, science hasn't stopped the story. As it goes, the Lady of the Lake travels back and forth, crossing the dark lake with her lover. But, unlike Drummond, for her there is no escape.

🚗 Chesapeake/Suffolk: Great Dismal Swamp National Wildlife Refuge

From High Street at Portsmouth, continue west on US-58 (Airline Blvd.) for 11.7 miles, briefly cutting through a small portion of Chesapeake (a city named for the Chesapeake Indians). Bear right at Suffolk's US-58 Business route exit and go 1.4 miles. Turn left on VA-337 (Washington St.) and go 0.7 miles east. Make a sharp left turn at VA-642 (White Marsh Rd.) and continue south, passing the Jericho Ditch entrance at 0.7 miles and the Washington Ditch/Dismal Town Boardwalk entrance after another 4.5 miles.

The Dismal Town Boardwalk, near Washington Ditch, stretches about a mile through the swamp. From here, continue south on VA-642 for one mile. Turn left on VA-604 (Hosier Rd.) and go 1.7 miles to the Great Dismal Swamp National Wildlife Refuge office, on the left. Trails follow roads through the swamp to Lake Drummond; maps are available at the refuge office. The lake lies in both Suffolk and Chesapeake. From the refuge headquarters, retrace the route to US-58 Business at VA-337.

Confederate Graffiti

After a fire tore down buildings across Suffolk in 1837, Mills Riddick insisted on using bricks to build his new home. Rising nearly four stories, with 16 fireplaces and 21 rooms, Riddick's mansion became a gargantuan sight. Neighbors jokingly called it "Riddick's Folly," saying that it was a folly to build such a massive Greek Revival structure.

But it proved perfect for Union Maj. Gen. John James Peck, who took over Riddick's Folly as a hospital and a headquarters for his staff of Army officers during the Civil War.

Peck arrived in Suffolk just a few months after Union troops of the First New York Mounted Rifles marched into town on May 12, 1862. The Union sent 29,000 troops to hold Suffolk, hoping their might would provide a buffer between the already-captured port cities of Norfolk and Portsmouth and the railroads leading west.

Then came trouble. Confederate forces under Gen. James Longstreet flanked the area in April 1863, laying siege to Suffolk. For nearly a month, Longstreet's forces kept the Union unable to move, until Longstreet withdrew on May 4, 1863, without an actual

Riddick's Folly, a Civil War site in Suffolk

battle. By the end of the summer, Peck had left Suffolk, too.

When the Union occupation was over, Riddick's son, Nathaniel, returned to the family home at Riddick's Folly. The younger Riddick found the mansion looted and stripped of its furnishings. Only a single chair remained. Riddick also found penciled messages all over the walls. Henry Van Weech, a cavalryman from New York, wrote "E Pluribus Union [sic]." There was also Confederate graffiti, saying: "Yanks you ought to be here / Know that we would give you a good time / Go home and stay there."

In his law office, Nathaniel Riddick discovered a mysterious message from Lt. Amos Madden Thayer, a signal officer in the Union Army. Thayer had used the office during the occupation and noted to Riddick his "great respect for the taste displayed in ornamenting your grounds."

But Thayer added, "I must confess that I believe the cause in which you are engaged decidedly wrong—We shall see however—I hope to meet you on friendly terms in more peaceful times and enjoy you socially."

🚗 *Suffolk: Riddick's Folly*

From VA-337 (East Washington St.), head west on US-58 Business for 2.5 miles, proceeding into downtown Suffolk. Just beyond the Suffolk Conference Center, turn left on Main Street. The Riddick's Folly House Museum, at 510 N. Main St., stands immediately on the left. The house is listed on historic landmark registers and is open for tours.

Peanut Capital of the World

Peanut Capital of the World

Mr. Peanut stands in Suffolk.

Mr. Peanut came out of his shell wearing a chef's hat. In another sketch, the cartoon goober carried a lunch box that said "Planters." Suffolk teenager Antonio Gentile created this hand-drawn character in 1916 and won five dollars when Mr. Peanut became the symbol of the Planters Nut & Chocolate Company.

Established in Pennsylvania, Planters moved its headquarters to Suffolk in 1913. At the time, similar peanut factories had been in operation among Suffolk's sprawling peanut farms. Peanuts had been grown commercially in Virginia since the 1840s, when Dr. Matthew Harris harvested a crop near Waverly.

Still, it took the vision of Planters founder Amedeo Obici—as a community leader, businessman, and philanthropist—to truly transform sleepy Suffolk into the "Peanut Capital of the World."

Much of Obici's success can be boiled down to his relentless marketing of Mr. Peanut. A commercial artist dressed the nut-shaped fellow with a top hat and monocle. Soon, Mr. Peanut showed up on product labels, in magazines, and on the backs of nut-shaped cars, called "Peanutmobiles," driven by Planters sales representatives.

Today, the character remains a fixture of Suffolk's parades and festivals, long after the deaths of Obici and Gentile. Likenesses of the debonair icon can also be seen all over the "Peanut Capital" and the world.

🚗 *Suffolk: Mr. Peanut*

From Riddick's Folly, follow Suffolk's Main Street into the downtown district for 0.6 miles. A three-foot-tall cast-iron statue of Mr. Peanut stands atop a granite monument at the Character Corner, where Main Street meets Washington Street. Here, a right turn leads 0.1 miles to the Planters Peanut Center, 308 W. Washington St. Turn left at the Character Corner, follow Washington Street for 0.2 miles, turn right on Hall Street, and then turn immediately left on Culloden Street to reach the Planters Peanut Factory, on the right. From Character Corner, retrace Main Street to rejoin US-58 Business near Riddick's Folly.

The Flood

Forecasts looked treacherous. Heavy winds and relentless rain clobbered the Carolina coast. And then? This storm took aim at a Virginia city that some say was named for Benjamin Franklin. The local newspaper issued a warning—"Region Braces for Floyd"—on September 16, 1999. But, by then, Hurricane Floyd had found Franklin and flooded it.

Water cascaded over concrete median walls dividing Franklin's US-58 Bypass while more than 180 downtown businesses stood in at least three feet of water. Some Franklin stores were lost in liquid deeper than an Olympic-size swimming pool. Coffins and concrete vaults floated out of the ground at cemeteries in nearby Southampton County. And the city park at Barrett's Landing simply slipped into submersion.

Franklin didn't exactly start on high ground. Surrounded by swamps, Franklin was settled in the 1830s at the head of navigation on the Blackwater River.

By the late 1800s, it had become the home of a paper mill, headed by Paul D. Camp and his broth-

Blackwater River at Barrett's Landing in Franklin

ers Robert and James. The business grew into Camp Manufacturing Company, later Union Camp Corporation, which ultimately became a parcel of International Paper Company.

The flood paralyzed operations. And, soon, rumors swirled like all that unwelcome water flowing out of the Blackwater River. Only months earlier, the paper plant had changed hands. Now, many guessed, Franklin's largest employer would be shuttered.

It took a week for both the floodwaters and rumors to recede. The paper plant reopened. In a few days, boats could no longer float over soggy streets. And, like a phoenix, Franklin rose again, surviving the greatest flood in the city's history—but, unfortunately, not its last. In 2006, history nearly repeated itself with another overflow in Franklin. This time, however, the waters did not rise as high, nor was the damage as devastating, as the event in 1999, a catastrophe still remembered by locals as simply "The Flood."

🚗 Franklin: Barrett's Landing

From Suffolk's Main Street at Riddick's Folly, turn left on US-58 Business and go three miles to rejoin US-58. Continue west for 8.5 miles to the Holland/Franklin exit. Proceed for 0.6 miles into Holland (named for early merchant Z. T. Holland). A monument stands on the right, paying tribute to the first Ruritan club, a civic organization that began here in 1928. A newspaper reporter, Daisey Nurney, invented the word *Ruritan,* using Latin terms to reflect the club's rural setting. From that monument, continue west on US-58 Business, passing through Carrsville (named for early settler Jonas Johnston Carr). At 10.5 miles beyond the Ruritan monument, reach the downtown district of Franklin. Turn left on Main Street and go through town to Barrett's Landing on the Blackwater River. From here, retrace Main Street for a half mile to US-58 Business (Fourth Ave.). Turn left and go five miles to rejoin US-58.

Go Into Jerusalem

Nat Turner had visions. The slave saw figures of white spirits and black spirits engaged in battle, and he found drops of blood on corn, as though it were dew. Turner also saw an eclipse in February 1831 and figured that was a sign from God—and a time to revolt.

By the end of the year, Turner and a band of fellow slaves turned Southampton County's cotton fields into killing fields. They beheaded men, women, and children. They axed every white body they found.

All told, Nat Turner's insurrection was the greatest slave uprising in the history of the United States. It inspired paranoia among slave owners and debates over the future of slavery. It also came at great surprise. Previously, there had been no sign of revolt among the slaves of Southampton County.

The insurrection leader, "Preacher" Nat Turner, was well liked and well treated. Born in 1800, Turner had convinced his followers that he had divine guidance. He had a plan to "go into Jerusalem," the courthouse town of Southampton County. There, Turner would gather more recruits, and the slaves would fight their way to freedom.

But first, Turner took another cue from the sun.

It appeared like a circular plane of polished silver on August 13, 1831. The atmosphere turned hazy, gloomy, and green. Turner saw this strange day as God's final message: his insurrection must begin.

Turner and his recruits marched into darkness, swinging swords and hatchets. On August 22, at two in the morning, the slaves crept into the house of Joseph Travis, Turner's master and a white man that Turner actually liked. Travis slept. Turner stabbed him, drawing the rebellion's first blood. Other slaves then slaughtered everybody else in the Travis house, even bashing out an infant's brains against a brick fireplace.

The killing continued. Plundering houses and littering lawns with bloody corpses, Turner's army enlisted other slaves to join the rampage. The runaways massacred at least ten students at a school for girls, and the force grew about tenfold with up to 60 slaves, many on horseback.

At the home of Nathaniel Francis, a three-year-old white boy stood in a lane, watching the slaves' horses. The little boy asked for a ride. He was picked up, beheaded, and tossed back to the ground. The boy's eight-year-old brother screamed, and he too was slashed to death.

This historic marker near Courtland notes Nat Turner's Insurrection.

Brandy turned the tide. At the home of James W. Parker, some of Turner's recruits rolled barrels of apple brandy into the yard and drank so much that they stopped to slumber in the shade. The slaves then encountered the county militia, armed with guns. Many slaves fled. Some even went home and said they had been forced to join the raid.

Turner's diminished force regrouped the next day. But at the home of Dr. Simon Blunt, some slaves turned on Turner's gang and defended their master. Troops moved in, and then the insurrection was over. By then, Turner's army had killed as many as 60 whites.

Turner somehow escaped. He eluded hundreds looking for him across Virginia, Maryland, and North Carolina. For weeks, reports arrived of his capture or whereabouts on the nearby Nottoway River, in the mountains near Fincastle, Virginia, or as far as the West Indies.

Several slaves were executed for participating in the rebellion. Vengeful white mobs, meanwhile, murdered as many as 200 free and enslaved blacks. The head of one black man was cut off and stuck on the "Blackhead Sign-Post" on the road to Jerusalem, a warning against any future insurrections.

All the while, Turner hid himself in dugouts. He had scratched one hole, what he called a "cave," under a pile of fence rails in a field, not far from where his rebellion began. Finally, at gunpoint, Turner was caught on October 30. Dragged into Jerusalem, he was put on trial and sentenced to die. Standing on a scaffold in his last moments, Turner promised it would grow dark and rain for the last time. And it did rain, followed by a drought.

Turner was hanged on November 11. His body was slashed and skinned. Oil was made from his flesh, and his skeleton was cast off for souvenirs.

The Southampton County Courthouse where Turner's trial was held is now gone. A new one was constructed at the same site in 1834. After 1888, the road taken by Turner no longer went into Jerusalem. The town was renamed "Courtland." Postmistress Fannie Barrett had suggested a new name was needed, saying residents were tired of people making annoying references to "Those Arabs from Jerusalem."

🚗 Courtland: Southampton County Courthouse & Nat Turner's Insurrection Marker

From the westernmost entrance to Franklin, continue west on US-58 for two miles. Veer right on US-58 Business at Courtland and pass the Southampton Agriculture and Forestry Museum (with exhibits related to local history, including Nat Turner's Rebellion), on the right at 26315 Heritage Lane. At two miles, reach the Southampton County Courthouse, on the left, and Mahone's Tavern, a historic landmark, on the right. Continue through town for another 2.5 miles. At Courtland's westernmost junction of US-58 Business and US-58 Bypass, go south on VA-35 for 7.7 miles to the Nat Turner's Insurrection historic marker.

From the marker, return north on VA-35 for 0.2 miles. Turn left on Cross Keys Road and go 1.4 miles. Turn right on Clarksberry Road (VA-668) and go two miles to the Cabin Pond Lane (VA-702) intersection. Nat Turner's Insurrection began in this vicinity. Retrace the route from Cabin Pond Lane: return two miles on Clarksberry Road (VA-668), turn left on Cross Keys Road and go 1.4 miles, then turn left on VA-35 and go 7.5 miles north to US-58.

Piedmont

Grassy hills frame farms on the outskirts of Lawrenceville, sidewalks connect quaint shops at Martinsville, and antique mansions line Millionaire's Row on Main Street in Danville. This is Virginia's Piedmont, also called "Southside" or simply "Southern Virginia."

It's a land revved-up with racetracks and hooked on hosting fishing tournaments at Lake Gaston and Buggs Island Lake. Virginia's longest road rolls through this pastoral region like a runway, connecting Emporia and Edgerton to South Hill and South Boston.

The Applejack Raid

I was just before Christmas, and a fresh batch of brandy waited in homes across Virginia. Farmers like Benjamin Bailey called this "applejack," and Bailey had about 25 barrels of it hidden under haystacks on his farm a few miles north of Hicksford.

Emporia's Village View Mansion dates to about 1795

Then came the march of the Civil War. In the snow and sleet of 1864, Union Maj. Gen. Gouverneur K. Warren headed south from Petersburg to Hicksford with more than 26,000 men. Warren wanted to destroy the section of the Petersburg and Weldon Railroad that ran between Stony Creek and Hicksford's Meherrin River bridge, a vital supply line to the Confederacy.

On December 7, Warren's troops followed the Jerusalem Plank Road but were spotted by Confederate scouts. Word reached Confederate leaders Maj. Gen. Wade Hampton, Maj. Gen. W. H. Fitzhugh Lee, and Capt. William H. Briggs, and they quickly devised a defense while meeting at the finest home in Hicksford, a circa-1795 mansion called "Village View."

Along the route, several Union soldiers stopped marching after finding some of the applejack hidden under Bailey's haystacks. Casually, these men from Maine threw a big party instead of heading south with the invasion. Scores got drunk, laughing and singing, and 43 wandered off, later to be listed as missing.

Then came gunfire on December 9. Bullets blasted Belfield, the small town that adjoined Hicksford along the Meherrin River. Confederate troops fired back, and five local boys voluntarily scuttled into the crossfire. The boys followed the Confederate plan to torch a wagon-road bridge. When that burned, the Union troops were cut off from moving farther south.

Warren withdrew on December 10 after his troops had destroyed more than 15 miles of the railroad and severed the Confederate supply line. While in retreat, Warren's troops ransacked homes across Sussex County, drinking more confiscated applejack and later prompting the Hicksford Raid (or Belfield Skirmish) to be comically called "The Applejack Raid."

The name "Belfield" came from developer Belfield Starke, who laid out the town in the 1790s. The original name of "Hicks Ford" came from an Indian trader, Capt. Robert Hicks, who had settled around 1709 along the Meherrin River, a watercourse named for a local Indian tribe. In 1887, the tiny towns of Belfield and Hicksford combined to form the singular city of Emporia, borrowing the new name from Emporia, Kansas.

🚗 Emporia: Village View

From the VA-35 junction at Courtland, go 23.5 miles west on US-58, passing through Capron (named for a railroad official) and Drewryville (named for a local Drewry family). Use the Emporia exit at US-58 Business and follow for 1.5 miles. Turn left on Main Street (VA-301) and go south for one mile. Turn left at Briggs Street and go 100 yards. Village View stands immediately on the left, beyond the railroad tracks at the Clay Street corner. Listed on historic landmark registers, the Federal-style house is sometimes open for tours. From Village View, retrace Main Street to US-58 Business and turn left. Go through Emporia for a half mile and then bear right on Market Drive to rejoin US-58 West.

Brunswick Stew

Stewmasters of Brunswick County would cook squirrel. They just can't find many. Over the past century or so, the natural squirrel population has been largely depleted. So they'll likely chop chicken, instead, when they stir early in the morning.

It's all for the Battle of the Brunswicks; both Brunswick County, Virginia, and Brunswick, Georgia, claim to be the birthplace of Brunswick Stew. The debate has even simmered into a "stew war," with contests pitting "stewmasters" of the Old Dominion against chefs from the Peachtree State. One skirmish actually ended in interstate controversy when the mayor of Brunswick, Georgia, walked away with a contest trophy after stealing it from the winning Virginians!

In the ladle of history, Georgia points to a statue of a stewpot and says the first Brunswick Stew was made in it in 1898 on St. Simon's Island.

Virginia's claim dates much earlier. In 1828, Dr. Creed Haskins went hunting with friends a few miles north of the Brunswick County Courthouse in Lawrenceville. A slave cook named Uncle Jimmy Matthews stayed in camp, shooting a few squirrels

Brunswick County welcomes travelers on US-58.

and skinning them. Matthews tossed the squirrels in a pot with some stale bread, butter, and onions. The returning hunting party liked eating his concoction so much that they tried making "Squirrel Stew" again.

Over the years, the thick stock has been renamed "Matthews Stew" (for Uncle Jimmy) and "Haskins Stew" (for the family that preserved the recipe). Cooks added tomatoes, corn, and butter beans, plus one slice of bacon and one small onion for each squirrel. Some cooks substitute rabbit for squirrel. Some say only lamb will do, instead of chicken, if enough squirrels cannot be found.

In 1988, the county's cooks brewed a big batch in Richmond, Virginia, and the Virginia General Assembly declared Brunswick County "the original home of Brunswick Stew."

The "Brunswick" name, by one theory, comes from the German duchy of Brunswick-Luneburg, one of the possessions of King George I. As for the "Lawrence" of Lawrenceville, one account says he was the favorite horse of Col. James Rice, who gave land for the site of the courthouse town. Another says the name honors Capt. James Lawrence, the naval hero who cried "Don't give up the ship" while aboard the *Chesapeake* during the War of 1812.

Brunswick County Museum in Lawrenceville

🚗 *Lawrenceville: Brunswick County Courthouse & Brunswick County Museum*

From the westernmost US-58 Business exit at Emporia, follow US-58 west for 17 miles, passing through Durand (named for an owner of the Atlantic and Danville Railroad), Bufford Crossroads (named for early settler Thomas Lawrence Buford), and Pleasant Shade (named for a large grove of trees). Turn right at the Lawrenceville exit on US-58 Business and go 1.6 miles to Lawrenceville's courthouse square. The Brunswick County Museum stands on the left, next to the circa-1853 courthouse. From here, continue for one mile west on US-58 Business to US-58.

Fort Christanna

Fort Christanna

Cannons boomed. It was 1716, and Royal Gov. Alexander Spotswood ceremoniously inspected Fort Christanna, a five-sided outpost built to improve trade relations between Indians and white settlers.

Prior to 1714, when Fort Christanna was established, some white settlers had grown infamous for getting local Indians drunk on rum and cheating them in business deals. But Spotswood's Virginia Indian Company tried to change that by regulating and restricting trading to the confines of the fort.

Spotswood had coined the name "Christanna" by combining the names of Jesus Christ and Anne, the Queen of England. Under the command of Capt. Robert Hicks of nearby Hicks Ford, Virginia, Fort Christanna could protect both settlers and local tribes against raids by the northern Iroquois and the Tuscaroras of North Carolina. The fort also included a school to teach Indian children the three R's plus Bible verses. Strategically, these same Indian children could double as hostages in case the fort was attacked.

Still, some Virginia leaders had argued against the company's monopoly on trade. Others simply suspected that Spotswood personally profited from the

A monument located near the site of Fort Christanna

enterprise. Ironically, the peace that the fort provided triggered its doom, starting with the dissolution of the Virginia Indian Company in 1717. Within months, Fort Christanna's organization became unclear, and rangers turned mutinous, refusing to stand guard.

Local Saponi Indians continued to live at Fort Christanna as late as 1729. But nearly all traces of the fort were gone by 1924, when a small cannon was erected as a monument to mark the site.

According to legend, three of Fort Christanna's original cannons were dumped at the bottom of the fort's well. A fourth was eventually moved to the Williamsburg campus of the College of William & Mary. A fifth was overstuffed with gunpowder in 1887 and exploded during an inauguration celebration for President Grover Cleveland at nearby Lawrenceville.

Brunswick County: Fort Christanna

From US-58 at Lawrenceville, continue straight on VA-46, going south, for 2.6 miles. Turn right on VA-686 (Fort Hill Rd.) and go 1.1 miles to a monument with a small cannon on the right. The actual Fort Christanna was located nearby. From here, retrace the route to US-58 West.

South of the Hill

There is no "South Hill"—much less a mountain—in Mecklenburg County. But a big hill standing northwest of town was once dubbed a "mountain." It even inspired the name "Mountain Creek" for a stream at its base.

A community near that "mountain" was called "South of the Hill" in the early 1800s. That moniker was soon shortened to "South Hill." Then that same name traveled to the post office of the present South Hill, which was previously called "Ridgefork."

Incorporated in 1901, South Hill was once literally a round town. Like Troutdale, Virginia, the municipality's boundaries formed a perfect circle, with a center spike pounded in the ground near the railroad depot.

In 1924, South Hill's original train station burned to the ground. The next station, made of bricks, literally went to the birds as a home to pigeons after being abandoned for several years. Renovated in the late 1980s, the South Hill Depot became a repository for two unlikely collections: model railroads and dolls.

Retired schoolteacher Virginia S. Evans donated the dolls, a 500-head collection ranging from Kewpie dolls of the 1920s to a likeness of Mr. Peanut. Ralph Schneider, a German shipbuilder, used old postcards for reference when he designed the depot's detailed model of the Atlantic & Danville Railway. Volunteers used green fiber, toothpicks, and hair spray to make a landscape of 10,000 little trees for the model.

The model railroad shows miniature versions of Clarksville, LaCrosse, and South Hill, all before 1967, the year South Hill's boundaries expanded beyond its original circle.

Possibly, the circle of South Hill meant more than anyone knew. It was just a line on the map. But maybe it could have been viewed from outer space, like a crop circle. At the least, it did seem strange when South Hill's C. N. Crowder reported seeing a UFO in the vicinity of the town's East Ferrell Street on April 21, 1967, just a few weeks after the town's new boundary was drawn.

Crowder said the UFO—with a 20-foot metal storage tank and legs about three and a half feet high—blasted off with white fire and left a burned spot on the road. Representatives of NASA investigated the incident. So did media representatives and curious sightseers, to little conclusion.

The South Hill Depot

🚐 *South Hill: South Hill Depot*

From the VA-46 junction, continue west on US-58 for 15.6 miles, passing through Brodnax (named for a local family that operated a large cotton market) and LaCrosse (named either for the crossing of two railroads, or the game lacrosse).

Turn right at South Hill on US-58 Business and go 1.1 miles. Turn left on Mecklenburg Avenue and go 0.2 miles to South Hill Depot, 201 S. Mecklenburg Ave. From South Hill Depot, follow through South Hill for three miles west on US-58 Business to rejoin US-58 West.

Boyd Town

Boyd Town

Alexander Boyd collapsed. Maybe it was a heart attack or maybe a stroke. But on August 11, 1801, Boyd suddenly fell over his judge's bench in a Mecklenburg County courtroom and died at age 54.

The well-liked leader left behind a namesake son. Only, this Alexander Boyd soon found foes. People said the younger Boyd held a monopoly in Mecklenburg County for owning the site of the county courthouse, part of the property inherited from his father.

To appease opponents, Boyd sold two acres to the county for $1 in 1811 and then conveyed 50 acres to create "Boyd Town," later called "Boydton." Still, Boyd grumbled, saying any attempt by others to remove the courthouse from his property would be "wanton confiscation."

Boyd's property included Boyd Tavern, a sprawling structure that once belonged to his father. Boyd spent big bucks enlarging this inn, built around 1790, and he served his guests liquor imported from Europe. But his finances collapsed, just like his father had. In 1824, he sold the tavern to William Townes, operator of Boydton's short-lived racetrack.

The tavern stayed a hospitality hot spot, especially

The Boyd Tavern at Boydton

for horse-racing participants. All gathered, winner or loser, for the hotel's lavish balls. But then, after 1832, all bets were off. Townes's racetrack became the site of Randolph-Macon College, and the tavern became a meeting place for students and professors.

During the Civil War, Confederate troops mustered outside Boyd Tavern. Randolph-Macon College, meanwhile, lost both students and professors to battlefields plus most of the school's endowment to worthless Confederate bonds. In 1868, the Boydton campus closed, and Randolph-Macon relocated to Ashland, Virginia, to be closer to a railroad.

Boyd Tavern remained. It survived a downtown fire in 1907 and a dynamite explosion used to stop its own fire in 1916. It also inspired vague legends of ghosts to explain its creaky floorboards and the mysterious voices heard in its basement. Restored as a community meeting place, the tavern's dollhouse-quality detail has been delicately preserved, especially on its fanciful front porch, which faces the grave of the elder Alexander Boyd.

Boydton: Boyd Tavern

From South Hill, continue west on US-58 for 12.7 miles. Turn left on US-58 Business, which runs through Boydton for 1.3 miles to another junction with US-58. The original campus of Randolph-Macon College stood near the corner of Jefferson and School streets. Boyd Tavern stands at the corner of Madison and Washington streets. Alexander Boyd's tombstone, in the lawn next to the Mecklenburg County Health Center, includes a poem explaining his death:

> Twas on the bench 'pon a court day / No doubt you will read with sorrow / For I was dead before the night / Prepare my friends to follow.

Rebellion on the Roanoke

Nathaniel Bacon cooked up a plan. The young lawyer had grown tired of the Susquehannock Indians who raided outposts on the Virginia frontier. And he was equally upset about Royal Gov. William Berkeley's failure to do much about it.

So Bacon went west with about 200 men in May 1676 and approached the Occaneechi Indians living at a four-mile-long island on the Roanoke River. The Occaneechi had a monopoly on furs, and they had a business association with Berkeley, trading animal skins.

Bacon convinced the Occaneechi to expel a band of marauding Susquehannocks. After that, something happened. No one knows exactly what, but stories say the Occaneechi refused to turn over their prisoners and plunder to Bacon. One of Bacon's men was shot. A two-day battle ensued, with Bacon slicing apart the Occaneechi village and killing an unknown number of the tribe. Bacon then took off with the Occaneechis' beaver pelts.

Virginians at the colonial capital of Jamestown hailed Bacon as a hero for fighting Indians. But an enraged Berkeley acted like he wanted to throw Bacon into a frying pan for waging war with the Occaneechi, his business partners. Berkeley deemed Bacon's action a rebellion on the Roanoke and said Bacon had no official commission to fight Indians.

Bacon, on the other hand, proved to be just as pigheaded as Berkeley. Backed by hundreds of followers, Bacon marched on Jamestown, protesting Virginia's high taxes and low prices paid for tobacco. He also demanded a commission to fight Indians. For safety, Berkeley fled Jamestown and sailed to Virginia's Eastern Shore.

With Berkeley gone, Bacon essentially took over the government. He issued a declaration citing Berkeley as a corrupt official who played favorites and protected the Indians for his own benefit. Then Bacon turned destructive. He burned the major buildings at Jamestown in September. About a month later, Bacon found himself fried with fatigue. He met a not-so-noble death, succumbing to dysentery in October 1676.

"Bacon's Rebellion" crumbled. More than 20 of Bacon's supporters were later tried and hanged, including William Carver, an early settler at Portsmouth, and William Drummond, the lone hunter

Wigwam replica at Occoneechee State Park

when candles on a Christmas tree sparked a fire that burned the plantation's 20-room mansion. The day after the fire, an article in the *Boydton Gazette* theorized: "The Plantation was destined to tragedy, being named for the famous Occoneechee Indians who were massacred on one of the nearby islands in 1676."

🚗 *Clarksville: Occoneechee State Park*

At Boydton, follow US-58 west for 7.8 miles, passing the Rudds Creek Recreation Area (with a boat ramp, picnic area, and swimming beach) on the right. Turn left at Occoneechee State Park. The 2,698-acre park on Buggs Island Lake includes a playground, picnic shelters, campground, boat ramp, fishing areas, hiking trails, visitor center, and the historic site of the Occoneechee Plantation. A wigwam replica at the park shows what the Occaneechi Indians might have used when they lived on Occaneechi Island (now under the waters of Buggs Island Lake).

whose name remains on the lake at the center of the Great Dismal Swamp.

The Occaneechi Indians who remained fled Virginia. Some returned in the early 1700s and lived at Fort Christanna, near Lawrenceville.

A century later, the nearby Occoneechee Plantation borrowed the tribe's name, but only until 1898,

Sir Peyton's Place

Sir Peyton Skipwith kept his love in the family. He married his late wife's sister and caused alarm among members of the clergy.

But wait—Sir Peyton loved his sister-in-law. Jean Miller was a liberated and progressive woman. She was born at Blandford, near what is now Petersburg, and spent her formative years as a teenager in Scotland. She learned business, literature, music, and gardening.

After marrying Sir Peyton in 1788, Jean became a "Lady" to match his "Sir," a title for being an English baronet, a rank just above a knight. The Skipwiths had four children, adding to the four that Sir Peyton already had with Lady Ann Miller, Lady Jean's older sister.

Near the banks of the Roanoke River, Sir Peyton built a magnificent mansion with stones quarried on-site. Largely completed in the 1790s, Sir Peyton's place was named "Prestwould," a word meaning "near the trees." The 10,000-acre plantation once employed hundreds of slaves for large-scale crop farming.

According to an oft-repeated legend, Skipwith had gambled in cards with William Byrd III to win the land to build the house. But members of the Prestwould Foundation—the caretakers of the landmark—have soundly dismissed that story as

Prestwould Mansion, near Clarksville

unfounded, insisting that the wealthy Skipwith paid for this tract of land.

The Skipwiths operated a ferry, shuttling passengers across the Roanoke River near Occaneechi Island. The ferry continued after Sir Peyton's death in 1805. But the widowed Lady Jean gained a reputation for watching her ferryboat operators like a hawk. She calculated exactly what a fare would bring and how many ferries should run each day.

Lady Jean's astute business sense kept Prestwould prosperous. The plantation was also glamorous, with the home's interior draped in custom wallpaper, fitted with Georgian woodwork, and lined with hundreds of books. Outside, rows of boxwoods, flowers, and fruit trees dotted Lady Jean's garden.

Fittingly, Lady Jean was laid to rest near that beloved garden, beside Sir Peyton. But, in death, Lady Jean created a mystery: her tombstone lists the year she died as 1826, but it fails to say what year she was born.

Clarksville: Prestwould Plantation

From the Occoneechee State Park entrance, go west on US-58 for a half mile. Turn north on US-15/VA-49 and follow for two miles. Turn left on Rt. 1601 and go a half mile to the entrance of Prestwould Plantation. Listed on historic-landmark registers, the mansion features many original furnishings and outbuildings, including a loom house, a smokehouse, an octagonal summerhouse, and a rare, 18th-century slave house. Prestwould is open for tours. From here, retrace the route to US-58 West.

Lake Country

Clarksville sat on the riverbanks awaiting the final flood. The little town had survived a fire in 1893 and decades of drunken, lazy ferryboat captains. Now, with a concrete dam built many miles downstream, Clarksville would watch its shoreline submerge into the ever-rising waters of the Roanoke River.

Far upstream from Clarksville, the Roanoke River tumbles out of the Allegheny Mountains near Christiansburg, Virginia. The river breaks through the Blue Ridge and rolls across Virginia in a rocky streak.

Then somewhere, between a dam at Smith Mountain Lake and the shores of Clarksville, the watercourse loses its identity. The name changes from "Roanoke," an Indian term meaning "shell money," to "Staunton," for Henry Staunton, who fought Indians on Virginia's Piedmont frontier.

No one has a clear answer for the name change. Perhaps early settlers didn't know the Staunton and the Roanoke was the same river, and that's how it got two names. But, beyond Clarksville, it becomes only "Roanoke" again and makes its way south to the Albemarle Sound, emptying near Roanoke Island, North Carolina.

Settlers and politicians talked in the late 1700s about taming this river. They wanted to clear its obstacles and create a navigable waterway. The Roanoke Navigation Company won a charter to do business in Virginia, and by 1816, much of the clearing work had been accomplished.

Anticipating traffic, places called Haskinton, Abbyville, and Springfield became ports for the tobacco trade in Mecklenburg County. Around the same time, a tavern owner named Clark Royster petitioned the Virginia General Assembly to form his own little village overlooking the river's Occaneechi Island.

Only, Royster didn't have a name for his town. Briefly, it was listed on a legislative bill as "Roanoke." In 1818, the settlement officially became "Clarksville," for Royster's first name.

Like his father, Royster operated a ferryboat, linking Clarksville to Mecklenburg's mainland. The Royster operation was one of several ferries crossing the river, but by the mid-1800s, James Sommervill had gained a monopoly on river traffic.

Sommervill's boats were notoriously messy. They leaked. Service was shoddy. One man, Eaton G. Field, had to pole a boat for a drunken ferryboat captain.

US-58 crosses Buggs Island Lake at Clarksville.

Another time, an inebriated captain fell out but was saved when a woman pulled him back in by his hair.

By 1905, a toll bridge connected Clarksville to the mainland. The ferry era ended, but the floods did not. In 1940, a rainy overflow killed three people, caused property damage amounting to millions of dollars, and drowned farm animals in their pastures. The river also flooded Occaneechi Island.

Immediately, talk turned beyond taming the river. The Army Corps of Engineers then began to study ways to turn 39 miles of the river into a reservoir.

The task would not prove easy. Cemeteries, schools, and houses had to be relocated. Hundreds of residents were told to move. According to legend, at least one survey crew was told to do the same when a woman brandished a shotgun, determined to keep her farm from the waters deep.

Congressman John Hosea Kerr of North Carolina fought to create this reservoir along the Virginia–North Carolina border. The new lake was named for him. But the dam's construction in the late 1940s was most commonly called the Buggs Island Project for its proximity to a wooded isle near Boydton once owned by Samuel Bugg.

Virginians loved Bugg. They loved the early settler's name better than Kerr's, at least. In 1952, when the dam was completed, Virginians rejected the official name, "John H. Kerr Reservoir." Instead, they insisted on "Buggs Island."

Today, the reservoir spreads across nearly 50,000 acres, making it Virginia's largest lake. Clarksville, in turn, became a gateway to Virginia's "Lake Country." But its shoreline changed dramatically: Clarksville's streets now start at "Second," since First Street slipped underwater in the final flood.

Clarksville: Buggs Island Lake

From US-15/VA-49, head west on US-58 Business for one mile across the Philip S. Julian Wilson Memorial Bridge to enter Clarksville. In crossing, look to the right, near the railroad trestle, to view the site of the flooded Occaneechi Island, several feet below the surface of the lake. At this point, both the east and west sides of the highway bridge are in Mecklenburg County, but the center actually rests in Halifax County, where the county border remains at the confluence of the Roanoke and Dan rivers. Reaching Clarksville, immediately cross Second Street, with a public access to the lake, on the left. From here, US-58 Business runs 2.5 miles through town until it rejoins US-58.

Fountain of Liquid Gold

Before Thomas F. Goode could turn the faucet on, he had to find it. The old spring that the locals had once loved the most at Buffalo Springs—the one that contained the mineral lithia—had become hidden in an overgrowth of brush. For a while, that lost spring flowed underground, emptying into a small tributary of Buffalo Creek in Mecklenburg County.

But Goode befriended an old woman, and, by using her memory, he learned the location of that nearly forgotten fount. Then he hooked that water into his bottling plant in Mecklenburg County, calling the source "Spring No. 2." The new spring joined the three that Goode had begun operating when he took over the Buffalo Springs Resort in 1874.

Goode made Spring No. 2 a fountain of liquid gold. The entrepreneur called it "Buffalo Mineral Water" and sold it across the United States, England, France, and Cuba in the 1880s. At that time, Virginia had grown famous for its Warm Springs, Hot Springs, and Healing Springs, all

places in Bath County, an area named for having so many baths of mineral spring water.

People once thought drinking mineral spring water, or bathing in it, would cure diseases of the throat, skin, and blood. That's why bottles of Goode's Buffalo Mineral Water boasted: "PHYSICIANS OF NATIONAL REPUTATION, both in the UNITED

The springhouse at Buffalo Springs is open to visitors.

STATES and in Europe have used this water, they have RENOWNED it as of GREAT VALUE and have RECOMMENDED it to their PATIENTS."

In 1811, John Speed operated a tavern at Buffalo Springs, named for the buffalo that once roamed the nearby hills. By the 1850s, a resort had grown with a hotel, a bowling alley, and a golf course. The place was later advertised as a safe haven from Civil War battle-fields. But alcohol was not allowed, leaving guests to rely solely on the springs to quench their thirst.

The popularity of Buffalo Springs dried up like other spring resorts across Virginia in the 1930s. Doctors no longer prescribed mineral water, and the Great Depression soaked up people's vacation money.

In 1947, the Buffalo Springs hotel building was dismantled when part of the resort was set to flood with the construction of Buggs Island Lake. The building was moved to a site on nearby US-58 and reopened as a nightclub, using names like "Club 58" and "The Greek Goddess." About 30 years later, the old hotel building mysteriously burned.

Buffalo Springs: Buffalo Springs Wayside

From the westernmost junction of US-58 and US-58 Business in Clarksville, follow US-58 west for 4.7 miles. Turn right on VA-732 (Buffalo Springs Rd.) and go 0.2 miles to the Buffalo Springs Wayside, on the left. A gazebo-style picnic shelter, like an old springhouse, stands near the once-famous Spring No. 2. Visitors can bottle the Buffalo Mineral Water for free. From the wayside, return along VA-732 to US-58.

Thrill of Berry Hill

In the antebellum South, James Coles Bruce had just about all the wealth in the world, with more than $1,000,000, hundreds of slaves, and a mansion that looked like a piece of Greece. But what he didn't have, after 1850, was his beloved wife, Eliza. And Bruce grieved to the point of lying on Eliza's grave and crying for her to come back to him.

For years, Bruce's emptiness prevailed, until he found himself exasperated by the downturns of the Civil War, and he died on March 28, 1865. Lying on his deathbed just two weeks before the war ended, Bruce said he knew that the lifestyles of wealthy plantation owners and slaveholders like himself would go to ruin at the end of the Civil War.

Bruce was born rich. His father, James Bruce, had struck gold with agricultural interests plus a chain of general stores across North Carolina and Virginia. In 1841, with his father gone, the younger Bruce acquired land to build a dream house for Eliza.

The couple's plantation, Berry Hill, once stretched across Halifax County as far east as present-day South Boston, a town named for Boston, Massachusetts, but dubbed "South" to distinguish it from Virginia's other Boston in Culpepper County.

James Coles Bruce made a great living on the out-

Berry Hill Mansion near South Boston

skirts of this tobacco town, overseeing crops at Berry Hill whenever he was not overseeing legislation as a member of the Virginia General Assembly. From 1842 to 1844, Bruce spent $100,000 building his 17-room Berry Hill mansion, which features stuccoed and whitewashed brick walls three feet thick, and eight Doric columns rising on the front porch, similar to the Parthenon of ancient Athens.

Bruce imported marble fireplaces from Italy, and he added false doors to the interior of the house simply for symmetry. He had silver-plated doorknobs and silver washstands in bedrooms. And, in the great hall, Berry Hill boasted its greatest architectural oddity—a horseshoe-shaped staircase built like it's floating, seemingly unsupported.

It all looks surreal, and, some say, spooky. The mansion eventually became the Inn at Berry Hill, a hotel offering luxurious accommodations. Still, the real thrill of Berry Hill must be tracking down its legendary apparitions, like the ghostly young boy wandering the great hall, or spirits dancing atop graves on the plantation lawn. Some people say they feel touched by something unseen as they walk the hotel's creaky floors or climb the steps of the floating staircase.

In 2005, Bell Captain Wyatt Barczak even reported seeing somebody walk "through" a door. "But I didn't hear any footsteps or anything," he said. "I just kind of caught it out of the corner of my eye."

Even more intrigue lies in the whereabouts of Berry Hill's silver. According to tradition, James Coles Bruce ordered his butler to bury a silver table service and washstands in case Union troops tried occupying the house. Some believe the silver fortune lies there still, buried somewhere on the plantation grounds.

South Boston: Berry Hill

From VA-732 near Buffalo Springs, follow US-58 west for 13.6 miles to US-501 at South Boston. Turn right on US-501 (not the truck route) and go north for four miles. Turn left on VA-654 and go 0.7 miles. Bear left on VA-659 when the road forks and go 1.3 miles. Turn right but remain on VA-659 for another mile to Berry Hill, 3105 River Rd., on the left. From here, retrace the route to rejoin US-58 West at US-501.

Note: The South Boston-Halifax County Museum, with local history displays, stands at 1540 Wilborn Ave.

Last Capitol of the Confederacy

Confederate President Jefferson Davis dashed off to Danville as Confederate Gen. Robert E. Lee went on the run. The year was 1865. Union forces had finally triggered the fall of the Confederate capital at Richmond. And Danville was as far south as Davis could go and still stay in Virginia.

Danville had been spared from Civil War battles but was plagued with wartime gloom. Six of Danville's tobacco warehouses had been converted into prisons, with thousands held captive, susceptible to starvation, dysentery, and disease. About 1,300 prisoners died in Danville in 1864 during a smallpox epidemic. Many prisoners had been shipped to town from overloaded confines in Richmond.

Now, on April 3, 1865, the Confederate government headed down to Danville, too.

Davis and members of his cabinet endured a journey of 140 miles. Taking 15 hours by rail, it would prove as terrifying as tiresome: the gov-

ernment train passed over busted-up tracks, and the floorboards of one railcar gave way near South Boston, sending at least five men to gruesome deaths, slaughtered by the crunch of the train's rolling wheels.

Finally, in Danville, Davis met Maj. William T. Sutherlin. A well-respected businessman, Sutherlin became Danville's mayor in 1855 and served as its chief wartime quartermaster, in charge of medicine,

Sutherlin Mansion in Danville

arms, and food supplies. With Davis's arrival, Sutherlin's stately mansion on Main Street became the last capitol of the Confederacy.

Davis stayed in a rear bedroom that had an escape route. He also held meetings with cabinet members and discussed options for carrying on the Confederacy. But Davis, really, could only wait and worry. He needed the protection of Lee's Army of Northern Virginia.

Just before leaving Richmond, plans had been made for the Confederate general to reach Danville, regroup, and keep fighting. Unfortunately, with communication lines cut, Davis had no way of knowing Lee's location.

On April 4, at the Sutherlin Mansion, Davis wrote what became his last official proclamation as president of the Confederacy. He acknowledged "the occupation of Richmond by the enemy," but to his citizens he promised: "it is my purpose to maintain your cause with my whole heart and soul; that I will never consent to abandon to the enemy one foot of the soil of any one of the States of the Confederacy."

The proclamation was grandiose and optimistic. And, yet, it was hardly reflective of the reality of both Davis and Lee in retreat.

Almost immediately, Davis turned to military matters and inspected earthwork fortifications surrounding Danville. He had once thought the town was defensible, in that the Union troops could be held back against the Dan River and nearby Staunton River. But he would conclude Danville's earthworks were "as faulty in location as construction."

Confederate troops built bigger fortresses. But Danville approached mild chaos—refugees overcrowded streets, hoping to be safe in the shadow of Davis's government.

On April 8, Davis finally received a direct word from Lee through a young messenger. Lee's army had suffered disastrously near Farmville at the Battle of Sailor's Creek. That news, unfortunately, was two days old. The next day, Lee surrendered his army to Union Gen. Ulysses S. Grant at Appomattox Court House.

The war was over. But it took a full day before Davis found out. At first, he sat in silence. Then he prepared to move again, still hoping to maintain the Confederate cause.

He thanked the Sutherlins for their hospitality. He bade farewell to the people of Danville. Then, in the darkness of April 10, 1865, Davis boarded a railcar. At little more than an hour before midnight, his train pulled out of sight.

🚗 *Danville: Danville Museum of Fine Arts and History*

From US-501 at South Boston, head west on US-58 for 30 miles, passing through Turbeville (named for its first postmistress, Mrs. Eugene C. Turbeville). Turn left on Danville's Main Street (VA-293) and cross the Dan River on the Martin Luther King, Jr. Bridge. Follow Main Street for one mile to the Sutherlin Mansion, on the left. Built in 1857, this Italian-villa-style house briefly served as a hospital during the flu epidemic of 1918 and, for years, was a public library. The mansion is now the Danville Museum of Fine Arts and History and includes Civil War exhibits and art collections.

Makin' Ninety Miles an Hour

Country music is all about love, heartbreak, and train wrecks. The latter actually helped the genre get started—a Danville disaster was turned into a million-selling hit by singer Vernon Dalhart. The song also stirred a fierce debate over its copyright.

Had it not been for that song, the 1903 crash of the "Old 97" would have gone down as just another train wreck. Instead, the song elevated—to mythic proportions—the story of engineer Joseph Andrew "Steve" Broady's attempt to make up for lost time. It captured the imagination of train enthusiasts. It even inspired the names of some Danville businesses.

On September 27, 1903, the express mail train No. 97 ran nearly an hour behind, with the delay possibly beginning with a wait for other cars at Washington, D.C. But it didn't matter where or when. The train would still be fined for not delivering mail on time.

So, quickly, Broady climbed aboard engine No. 1102 at Monroe, Virginia, and headed train No. 97 south toward Spencer, North Carolina. Broady was a substitute driver, but he had steered trains on this line before. Briefly, he stopped at the train station in Lynchburg. Then, in a rush, he took off again with 17-year-old Wentworth Armistead still on board. Armistead, a station employee, had jumped on the train only to lock the safe.

After making another stop for water at what is now Gretna, Virginia, the train continued rolling through Pittsylvania County. Its speed grew to about 55 MPH, maybe more. At any rate, it was too fast for Broady to safely approach the curved Stillhouse Trestle, standing 45 feet above a ravine north of Danville's downtown.

The locomotive whistle moaned long and loud. And No. 97 derailed, taking a nosedive at 2:42 P.M. The runaway train flew for more than 75 feet, and the locomotive landed on its top. Dust clouds rose out of the ravine, and canaries fluttered out of cracked cages in a wrecked cargo car, all on an otherwise quiet Sunday afternoon.

Hundreds raced down the hillside to the horrible scene of the dead and injured, scalded by steam. Broady died as skin peeled from his body. Armistead died too, but his remains were not immediately found. All told, eleven people were killed and six were injured.

Before long, writers began penning songs and poems about the eerie disaster. In 1924, the mangled

The "Old 97" is remembered in a Danville mural by Wes Hardin.

mess of the wreck rose out of the ravine and onto store shelves with records by Henry Whitter and Vernon Dalhart. Both singers borrowed the tune of a folk standard, "The Ship That Never Returned." Some say Dalhart borrowed, or just plain copied, the words from Whitter's earlier recording. Still, it was Dalhart's version of "Wreck of the Old 97" that sold more than 6,000,000 copies. It was also Dalhart's success that spurred a series of complicated copyright claims over who actually wrote the song.

Legends about the wreck also grew, largely because various versions of the song changed facts, like elevating the speed of the train to "makin' ninety miles an hour." A state highway historic marker also listed the wrong number of casualties, based on premature reports.

Broady's body was taken from the wreck and buried more than 100 miles away at Blackwell, Virginia, between Abingdon and Saltville. Today, the ravine lies overgrown with brush. Still, mysteries remain about the engineer's last moments and his tragic attempt to, as the old song goes, "put her in Spencer on time."

🚐 Danville: "Old 97" Mural & Wreck Site

From the Danville Museum of Fine Arts and History, retrace the route on Main Street for 0.7 miles to the Memorial Drive intersection. To the left, a mural by Wes Hardin depicts the "Old 97" story on the side of the Atrium Furniture & Design Center at the corner of Main Street and Memorial Drive. From here, continue for 0.3 miles on Main Street to US-58 Business (Riverside Dr.). Turn left and go 0.4 miles to a historic marker on the left, next to a convenience store, immediately west of the intersection of Highland Court and Riverside Drive. The train derailed immediately south of US-58 and crashed in the ravine. The Stillhouse Trestle and the train tracks are no longer in place.

Give Me Leatherwood!

Just four years after shouting "Give me liberty or give me death!" at St. John's Church in Richmond in 1775, Patrick Henry stood at the edge of the frontier, overlooking the Blue Ridge. Who knows, Henry might have then shouted "Give me Leatherwood!"

For five years, Henry's Leatherwood Plantation provided liberty with its remote location. It might have also saved him from death as he suffered bouts with malaria.

Starting in 1776, Henry served three consecutive one-year terms in Williamsburg as Virginia's first non-royal governor. But by 1779, with the American Colonies embroiled in war against England, he simply wanted peace, in the woods.

He had been west before. In the late 1760s, Henry tromped through the unsettled Holston Valley of Virginia and into present-day Kingsport, Tennessee. He roamed mountains while speculating on land with his brother William and his brother-in-law William Christian. The trip excited Henry's imagination.

So it might have seemed only natural that Henry would have gone to such a sparsely settled spot as Leatherwood in newly formed Henry County, which was named in his honor. He sold off Scotchtown, his house near Ashland, Virginia, and bought his 10,000-acre Leatherwood Plantation along the twisted course of Leatherwood Creek.

Back then, it was quite a summer's journey to what Henry called his "retirement," traveling with about 50 people, including his wife, newborn baby, older children, and a son-in-law, plus several slaves. Leatherwood stood 180 miles, or about a week away, from Richmond, where the state capital had recently moved from Williamsburg.

The Henrys had to initially clear their Leatherwood land of several squatters who had planted cabins in the plantation's hollows. Next, they built a two-room brick home and planted tobacco. They also grew enough corn to help feed American troops needing supplies after crossing the Dan River near present-day South Boston in 1781.

Only, Henry wasn't always around. He kept getting appointed or elected or simply suggested for political office. He turned down a chance to serve in Congress, but he accepted a bid in 1780 to join Virginia's House of Delegates. Still, plagued by poor health, he served only a few days.

The Patrick Henry Monument, near Axton

By the end of 1780, Henry found himself among other politicians, serving in the Virginia General Assembly. His "retirement" at Leatherwood languished. He championed the cause of defending America's frontier. He also successfully sponsored a bill to clear the Roanoke River and make it a navigable waterway.

Elected Virginia's governor again in 1784, Henry left Leatherwood and moved to Chesterfield County, near Richmond. About a dozen years later, he finally found his retirement at Red Hill at Brookneal, Virginia, his last home and where he was buried in 1799.

Henry's Leatherwood home no longer stands, but his name remains on places across his namesake county, including a community college, a bank, a real estate development, an insurance agency, and the Patrick Henry Mall. In 1790, his name was also used when forming Patrick County, giving Henry the honor of being the only person to have two of Virginia's counties named for him.

🚗 Axton: Patrick Henry Monument

From the Wreck of the Old 97 historic marker at the center of Danville (0.4 miles west of the Dan River bridge on Main St.), follow US-58 west for 21.6 miles, passing through Brosville to reach Axton (named for a local congressman's home, the Axton Lodge). Turn left on VA-620 (Old Liberty Dr.) and follow for 2.2 miles to the ten-foot-high Patrick Henry monument, on the right, marking the site of Patrick Henry's Leatherwood Plantation. A plaque on the boulder, erected in 1922, lists Henry's time in Henry County as "1778 to 1784." From here, retrace VA-620 to US-58. Turn west and go 1.7 miles to a historic marker, located at the entrance to Patrick Henry Farms at Rt. 1095 (St. Johns Circle). This marker stands 0.2 miles east of US-58's easternmost junction with US-58 Business at Martinsville.

Elephant Power

When John Fogerty sang, "They point the cannon at you" in Creedence Clearwater Revival's "Fortunate Son," he wasn't singing about Martinsville, Virginia. But he could have been, looking at the imposing cannons on the front steps of the old Henry County Courthouse.

Since the 1920s, these ten-foot-long iron cannons have pointed at the uptown portion of Martinsville, a city known since 1947 for all the horsepower under the hoods at Martinsville Speedway, its NASCAR track. Once at the courthouse, however, all spectators turned to the power behind elephant trunks.

The cannons—a pair of 19th-century naval guns—arrived by train from Fort McHenry, Maryland, a gift to Martinsville by the federal government. But they proved too heavy to be moved by conventional horsepower. So those cannons simply lay beside the train station, in the mud.

Later, a circus stopped in town, and the cannons were finally dragged from the train depot to the courthouse square with elephant power. The weapons have since proven an intimidating sight on the lawn of the old courthouse, even though the barrels are full of cement.

Cannon at the Old Henry County Courthouse

Dating to 1824, the old Henry County Courthouse was rebuilt in 1929 at the center of Martinsville, a city named for Gen. Joseph Martin. Like his contemporary Patrick Henry, Martin settled along Leatherwood Creek in Henry County. Martin also served in the Virginia General Assembly in the 1790s, representing the Henry County region.

🚗 *Martinsville: Old Henry County Courthouse*

Immediately west of Rt. 1095 (St. Johns Circle), continue west into Martinsville on US-58 Business for five miles. Bear right on Church Street at the Starling Avenue intersection and go 0.3 miles. Turn right on Clay Street, then immediately turn left on Main Street and go 0.3 miles to the Old Henry County Courthouse, on the right.

From the courthouse square, continue straight for 0.1 miles. Turn left on Moss Street and go one block. Turn left on Church Street and go 0.7 miles. Turn right on US-58 Business (Starling Ave.) and follow for 2.3 miles to rejoin US-58-Bypass on the west side of Martinsville, on the right. Martinsville Speedway lies on the south side of the city, off US-58-Bypass. Martinsville's Virginia Museum of Natural History, with multifaceted exhibits, stands at 21 Starling Ave., along US-58 Business.

Blue Ridge

Climbing into Patrick County, Virginia's longest road becomes the "Crooked Road," a driving trail connecting the musical hot spots of Virginia's Blue Ridge Highlands. This scenic area's name comes from early explorers who found a haze over the highlands that appears blue at a distance.

Here, trout streams tumble into tiny waterfalls, and Christmas trees grow at ear-popping elevations. Bluegrass music also comes alive, from Galax to Whitetop, as US-58 curls, climbs, and becomes quite crooked, indeed.

Tragedy on Tobacco Road

Abram Reynolds must have thought he was in high cotton. Why, he had gone down to North Carolina and had done just what his father, Hardin Reynolds, told him. He traded beans, flour, and apples. Then the 15-year-old boy returned to Virginia, ready to restock his family's country store.

Trouble was, Abram's newly gotten cotton had come from mills on the Deep River that had been quarantined for smallpox.

Hardin went haywire. Having heard of North Carolina's deadly smallpox outbreak and fearing for his family, he hastily vaccinated his children, at a risk. In 1862, vaccinations were not always considered safe.

It turned into tragedy. In less than a week, three of the Reynolds children died—two boys and a girl, all under the age of seven, all suffering the aftereffects of the vaccine. But an older boy, 12-year-old Richard Joshua Reynolds, the one they called "Dick," rushed outside and allegedly saved himself by washing vaccine off his arm in Rock Spring at the Reynolds Homestead in Patrick County.

Abram, still upset by the tragedy, enrolled at Virginia Military Institute. He then joined the Confederate Army, became a major in the Civil War, and accompanied Confederate President Jefferson Davis from Richmond to Danville in 1865. Abram considered going farther south with Davis as the war ended. But first he rode his horse to the Reynolds Homestead.

Hardin enthusiastically embraced his wayward son. "The Yankees have been here and torn up everything, and my Negro men have all gone with them," Hardin told Abram. "But, since you have come back alive and well, it is all right. We can rebuild our lost fortune."

The Reynolds family had amassed its fortune by manufacturing raw tobacco. That success was due to Hardin's thrift and industriousness, along with the help of the young Reynolds boys.

Abram joined his father as a business partner in 1867. Three years later, younger brother Dick showed up as a salesman, carrying tobacco products on a wagon.

Trouble was, Abram didn't always like how his little brother did business along the Tobacco Road.

Once, Dick had such bad luck making cash sales in the post-war economy that he simply bartered off a load of tobacco worth $2,000. He came home with a wagon piled with animal skins, beeswax, ginseng, furniture, and a gold watch. Abram was not pleased. Then Dick held an auction. As it turned out, he earned about 25 percent more cash from the auction's proceeds than he would have by selling the tobacco.

Abram—known as Major A. D. Reynolds—went west in 1872 to Bristol, Tennessee, and started a tobacco company that eventually employed about 500 people. He sold it in 1897 and died in 1925.

Dick—known as R. J. Reynolds—left home in 1874 for what is now Winston-Salem, North Carolina. He too started his own tobacco company, and it grew into nothing short of an empire, selling such products as Camel cigarettes, and employing as many as 10,000 people by the time of his death in 1918.

A younger brother, Hardin Harbour Reynolds, also took up business along the Tobacco Road. Born in 1854, Harbour became a business partner with his father in 1876. Later, Harbour promoted his own brand of chewing tobacco, Red Elephant, as having 1,000 spits to the chew.

Harbour worked in Bristol for Abram. He also had his own tobacco factory. But when that factory at South Boston went up in flames, Harbour returned to Patrick County to live with his wife and children at the Reynolds Homestead.

There would be more tragedy on Tobacco Road. In 1912, Harbour's six-year-old daughter, Nancy, awoke

Reynolds Homestead in Patrick County

early and reached for her Christmas stocking on the fireplace mantel. Her nightgown caught fire, and she died after deeply inhaling the flames.

Critz: Reynolds Homestead

From the westernmost junction of US-58 and US-58 Business at Martinsville, follow US-58 west for 17 miles, passing through Spencer (named for the family of first postmaster Peter D. Spencer) and Penns Store (named for a local Penn family that operated a store and tobacco factory). Turn right on VA-626 and follow for 3.3 miles, passing Critz (named for early settler Haman Critz, Sr.). Turn left at VA-798 (Homestead Lane) to enter the Reynolds Homestead. Built in 1847, the brick home is listed on historic landmark registers and is open for tours as a museum operated by Virginia Tech.

A Boy Named James

Even as a nine-year-old boy, James Stuart wouldn't let a sting knock him out of action. As his brother William Alexander ran for cover in a swarm of hornets, James just stood on a tree branch, taking swats until a huge hornet nest lay on the ground below him.

It was a sweeping skirmish, maybe even foreshadowing the battles that James would later lead as a great Confederate cavalryman, a time when he was known as "Jeb" Stuart. However, James wasn't called "Jeb" on Laurel Hill in Patrick County. Born on February 6, 1833, he was simply a boy named James, the seventh child and youngest son of Archibald and Elizabeth Stuart.

The "Jeb" nickname, formed from the initials of his name, James Ewell Brown, would come much later, in the 1850s, when red-haired Jeb became known for his jokes and singing. Stuart, also, was quite cavalier, wearing a red cape, knee-high boots, bushy beard, and an ostrich plume in his hat.

Stuart learned to ride a horse while on the family farm at Laurel Hill, several miles south of the Patrick County Courthouse. The Stuarts lived so close to North Carolina that their mail came from Mount Airy. But their neighborhood, called "The Hollow," was really part of Ararat, Virginia, named possibly for a Tarratt family, maybe the Indian word *tarraratt,* or perhaps Mount Ararat, the peak where Noah's Ark landed after the Great Flood.

For the Stuarts, a defining moment would be the

Laurel Hill monument at Ararat

great fire. It ripped down the family's wooden farm-house during the winter of 1847–1848, and they were left to live in a detached kitchen.

Before the fire, Stuart attended school in Wytheville, Virginia, living with his namesake uncle. He later enrolled at Emory & Henry College, graduated from the United States Military Academy at West Point, and served in the Army.

Just after the outbreak of the Civil War, he joined the Confederate Army and became the eyes of Gen. Robert E. Lee, serving as cavalry commander in the Army of Northern Virginia. In 1862, Stuart and his 1,200 men rode around Union Gen. George McClellan's entire 100,000-man Army of the Potomac. Stuart lost only one man in the action and supplied Lee with valuable information.

Still, with bodies piling up on battlefields, it was only natural that Maj. Gen. J. E. B. Stuart questioned his mortality. He told his wife, Flora, to prepare for the worst. He also longed for his "dear old hills" of home in Patrick County. In 1863, he wrote, "I would give anything to make a pilgrimage to the old place, and when this war is over quietly spend the rest of my days there."

He never got the chance. Laurel Hill was sold out of the family in 1859. Then, on May 11, 1864, Stuart was mortally wounded near Ashland, Virginia. A Union soldier from Michigan buzzed out of a nest of Federal troops and took a swat at him. Stung by a shot in his side, Stuart had to be pulled off his horse by his men.

Confederate President Jefferson Davis showed up in Richmond at Stuart's deathbed. Flora Stuart arrived on May 12, but it was too late. Stuart was gone, dead at age 31.

Major General J. E. B. Stuart

Patrick County's courthouse town gave up its name for the general. Once called Taylorsville for 18th-century settler George Taylor, the name changed to Stuart in 1884.

Stuart/Ararat: Patrick County Courthouse & Laurel Hill

From the US-58 junction at VA-626, follow US-58 west for 7.4 miles, passing through Patrick

Springs (the site of a springwater resort in the early 1900s). Turn left at the Stuart exit on US-58 Business (E. Blue Ridge St.) and go west for 0.7 miles to the Patrick County Courthouse, with a monument on the lawn dedicated to J. E. B. Stuart.

To reach Laurel Hill, turn left at the courthouse on North Main Street (Rt. T-1009) and go through town, veering left as the road turns to South Main Street and joins VA-8 (Salem Hwy.) After four miles, turn right onto VA-103 (Dry Pond Hwy.) and go 8.7 miles, passing through Claudville (named for a congressman, Claude Augustus Swanson). Turn right on VA-753 and go 10.6 miles to Laurel Hill, on the right.

The 75-acre Laurel Hill tract is unique because it is listed on historic landmark registers even though no historical structures exist on the site. From Laurel Hill, retrace the route to the Patrick County Courthouse at Stuart. Then turn left on US-58 Business to immediately reach the Patrick County Historical Museum, 116 W. Blue Ridge St., with displays related to J. E. B. Stuart. From the museum, US-58 Business runs one mile west to rejoin US-58.

Fairy Stones

Long ago, fairies frolicked, dancing beside a spring. Then came news from an elfin messenger: Jesus Christ, the Son of the Great Creator, had been crucified. The fairies cried, shedding tears that turned into "fairy stones" shaped like St. Andrew's, Roman, and Maltese crosses.

This story is, quite literally, a fairy tale. And scientists dismiss it, saying fairy stones are actually brown staurolite, a combination of iron, silica, and aluminum. When subjected to great heat and pressure, these minerals crystallize to form a cross. Possibly, the inch-long oddities called "cross rocks," "fairy stones," or "fairy crosses" were formed when the earth's plates shifted and pushed up the Blue Ridge Mountains.

Fairy stones are found in only a few places, like Fairy Stone State Park in Patrick County, along parts of the New River in North Carolina, and near the Blanchard Dam in Fannin County, Georgia. One tale says the Cherokee formed these cross rocks as they were pushed from their ancestral homes on the Trail of Tears.

In Virginia, Patrick County's fairy stone fields once belonged to Julius B. Fishburn, a Roanoke newspaper publisher. Fishburn was a partner at Fayerdale, an iron-mining town in the early 1900s located at the present site of Fairy Stone State Park. Fayerdale, the name now used by the state park's conference center, was formed by combining geologist Frank Ayer Hill's first initial and middle name with the middle name of another business partner, H. Dale Lafferty.

Fishburn donated 4,868 acres to create the park.

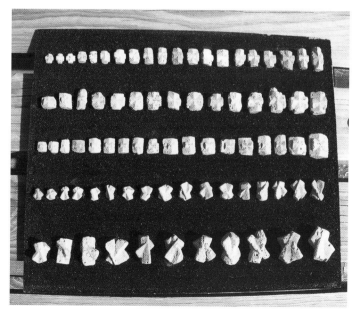

Fairy stones vary in shape and size.

The entrance to Fairy Stone State Park

It opened in 1936 as one of the first six state parks in Virginia. Contrary to popular belief, however, fairy stones cannot be found all over the park; only a small vein runs through a corner of the grounds.

President Teddy Roosevelt and inventor Thomas A. Edison both carried fairy stones. Legend says wearing them wards off witchcraft, sickness, accidents, and disaster. Fairy stones have also crossed into literature; they are portrayed as a symbol of luck and love in John Fox, Jr.'s 1908 novel *The Trail of the Lonesome Pine.*

Patrick County: Fairy Stone State Park

From the westernmost entrance of US-58 Business at Stuart, follow US-58 west for two miles. Turn right at VA-8 (Woolwine Hwy.) and go 3.9 miles north. Bear right on VA-57 and continue north for 7.7 miles. Turn left on VA-346 and go one mile to Fairy Stone State Park, featuring a campground, beach, fishing lake, playground, hiking trails, visitor center, and cabins. To reach the park's Fairy Stone Hunt Site, retrace VA-346 to VA-57, then turn left and follow VA-57 north for 2.7 miles. The hunt site is on the left, next to a small store.

Kissing Bridges

Walter G. Weaver concentrated on caskets. That's what he made, mainly. But Weaver also designed a couple of covered bridges. He even built the Bob White Bridge, which spans the Smith River.

Lovers loved it. Courting couples would stop a buggy in the bridge and carve their initials on the wooden walls. Some smooched. Naturally, covered bridges became "kissing bridges" and also "wishing bridges," since it was tradition to make a wish as you passed through.

Some believe bridges were covered so that horses would not get spooked as they crossed water. Actually, covered bridges had roofs simply to protect floorboards from rot.

Covered bridges are rare. About 100 once stood in Virginia. Fewer than ten now remain, and more than half, ironically, are located close to each other, with three in Giles County, all near Newport, and two in Patrick County, both near Woolwine. Virginia's oldest covered bridge, the 1857 Humpback Bridge near Covington, arches 100 feet over Dunlap Creek on the headwaters of the James River.

When Weaver constructed the 80-foot-long Bob White Bridge in 1921, he made it into a family affair. One of Weaver's sons helped with carpentry. Another poured cement. A daughter brought lunches to the work site.

The Weavers built the bridge to reach the Smith River Church of the Brethren. No one really knows for sure, but the Bob White Bridge and the long-

Bob White Bridge near Woolwine

Jack's Creek Bridge in Patrick County

River. Constructed in 1914–1916 by Charles Vaughan, the bridge was named because it leads to Jack's Creek Primitive Baptist Church.

Who was Jack? Perhaps he was the same boy who went up the hill to fetch a pail of water. Consider this: the rippling waters of Jill Creek join Jack's Creek about a mile north of the Jack's Creek Bridge.

🚗 *Woolwine: Bob White Bridge & Jack's Creek Bridge*

From the entrance road at Fairy Stone State Park at the VA-346 intersection, return south on VA-57 for 7.7 miles. Turn right on VA-8 and go 3.7 miles north. Turn left at VA-615 and go 0.1 miles to Jack's Creek Bridge, on the right. Then retrace VA-615 to VA-8, turn left and go 0.8 miles north. Turn right on VA-618 and go one mile to a right turn on VA-869, which leads about 200 yards to the Bob White Bridge. Both bridges are closed to vehicular traffic but open to pedestrians. From the Bob White Bridge, return to US-58 by retracing the mile on VA-618. Turn left and follow VA-8-South for 8.4 miles to US-58.

gone Bob White Post Office were both possibly named for the traditional "bob white" song of the area's quail.

Nearby, Weaver also designed the Jack's Creek Bridge at Woolwine, a Patrick County community named for its first postmaster Thomas B. Woolwine. Still, that landmark's name is misleading, since the Jack's Creek Bridge spans 48 feet across the Smith

Virginia Is for Leaping Lovers

Virginia Is for Leaping Lovers

All over the Old Dominion, so many cliffs are called Lovers Leap, you might figure the state's motto should be "Virginia Is for Leaping Lovers."

Lovers Leaps are perched at Whitetop Mountain, Natural Tunnel State Park, Jump Mountain near Lexington, and along Johns Creek near New Castle. One hugs the Shenandoah River in Clarke County, not far from Berryville. Another pierces the lip of the Breaks Canyon in Dickenson County.

Like all the others, the 3,300-foot-high Lovers Leap of Patrick County boasts a long-standing legend of a boy and a girl, each from warring Indian tribes. These lovers, forbidden to be together, play a fatal game of jumping into the afterlife, probably hoping to wake up on a star somewhere in each other's arms. For sure, if you jumped into the jungle below Patrick County's Lovers Leap, you would see stars—from toppling

into treetops and bouncing off outcrops while flying fast into the Smith River Valley.

Patrick County's original Lovers Leap lies on private property. What is now called Lovers Leap is a nearby public wayside. But it also boasts a grand overlook. And it stands between some suggestively

Patrick County's Lovers Leap Overlook along US-58

named geography, with Spoon Mountain on the east and Naked Ridge on the west.

A sign at the Lovers Leap wayside says it's unlawful to vandalize or deface public property. But love is blind. So have a heart for all those blind-eyed scribes, spray-painting and scratching this wayside's wall with proclamations: "Tammy + Bill," "Carol Loves Larry," or "Fay Hartless and Ben Fields 2gether 4-Ever." At least the graffiti seems patriotically applied in red, white, and blue. The colors even contrast, beautifully, when sunset's orange creams into crimson.

Patrick County: Lovers Leap

From the VA-8 junction west of Stuart, head west on US-58 for 5.4 miles as the road makes a steady ascension to Lovers Leap wayside, on the right. The Fred Clifton Park lies immediately west of the wayside, with picnic tables, grills, and short trails leading to scenic overlooks in a garden of rhododendron.

Dan River's Little Lighthouse

Dan River's Little Lighthouse

Virginia lighthouse lists never mention the stone sentinel at the headwaters of the Dan River, roughly 300 miles from the sea. Just 12 feet high, this little lighthouse once stood guard over the watercourse of the *Dan River Queen,* a side-wheeler paddleboat that Shirley Mitchell operated during the 1960s on the ten-acre Cockram Millpond.

Tourists loved to cruise on the 52-foot-long boat. One poor couple with very little money came here on their honeymoon and pretended to be on a fancy cruise ship. Others waved at the pond's birds and animals living near the lighthouse on a little island.

Mitchell spent a fortune constructing this place. He also lost a fortune. Nearby, he operated the Circle M Zoo with elephants, hyenas, buffalo, and monkeys, all shown to visitors on bus safari tours.

Over time, the lighthouse remained, but the boat and the zoo disappeared. The Cockram Milldam broke in 1989, and the pond turned into wetlands. The *Dan River Queen* was sold for salvage.

Then along came Sharoll Shumate. In 1999, this world-traveling motivational speaker bought the property near the Blue Ridge Parkway and used part of the 1884 Cockram Mill to open a pizza par-

Stone sentinel at Meadows of Dan

lor. Shumate also built an ice cream shop for "swingers"—a place where patrons sit on swings hanging from the ceiling. Shumate's plans to establish a resort and turn a rock quarry into a concert hall sounded ambitious for tiny Meadows of Dan, maybe even reminiscent of the late Shirley Mitchell.

But Shumate disproved doubters by 2001. He discovered the whereabouts of the long-lost *Dan River Queen* and hauled the hull home. Then he won a lengthy struggle with state environmental regulations to refill the pond: Dan River's little lighthouse could shine over water again.

Meadows of Dan, a community near the Blue Ridge Parkway

🚗 *Meadows of Dan: Cockram Mill*

From the Lovers Leap wayside and Fred Clifton Park, continue west on US-58 for 4.5 miles, passing through Vesta (named for the Greek goddess of the hearth). The Cockram Mill, named for former owner Walter A. "Babe" Cockram, stands on the right at a development called Blue Ridge Passage Resort. The lighthouse stands a few yards from the mill, near the

Dan River Queen. The mill is listed on historic landmark registers.

Cockram Mill marks the eastern gateway to Meadows of Dan, a scenic area with gift shops near the Blue Ridge Parkway. The community lies along meadows at the head of the Dan River, a watercourse that took its name either from a Saura Indian chief called "Danaho" or as a reference to the ancient tribe of the Danites, as told in the Bible's Joshua 19:47.

King Neptune stands over the Virginia Beach Boardwalk.

Atlantic Ocean at Cape Henry

Virginia Beach Fishing Pier

Barrett's Landing on the Blackwater River in Franklin

Sunset over Buggs Island
Lake at the site of the
flooded Occaneechi Island

Mabry Mill, the most photographed place on the Blue Ridge Parkway

Mayberry Trading Post stands along the Blue Ridge Parkway, slightly south of US-58.

New River near Bridle Creek, a popular canoe path along US-58. This stretch of the river was once slated to become part of a lake in the 1970s.

Musical roots run deep at Galax, the "World's Capital of Old-Time Mountain Music."

Natural overlooks afford long-range views at Grayson Highlands State Park.

Wild ponies roam the Mount Rogers National Recreation Area.

The Appalachian Trail winds along the base of Wilburn Ridge in the Mount Rogers National Recreation Area.

Snow falls often at Whitetop in Grayson County, a place famous for its Christmas tree farms.

Whitetop Laurel Falls splashes below the Virginia Creeper Trail near Damascus.

Copper Creek Trestle stands near the Clinch River at Clinchport.

Mountains enclose the scenic valley of Rye Cove in Scott County.

Overlooking Lee County, near Stickleyville, from atop Powell Mountain on US-58

Natural Tunnel in Scott County

The Real Mayberry

The Real Mayberry

Lizzie DeHart Mabry worked for years alongside her husband, Edwin Boston Mabry, a stout man known to all as "Uncle Ed." He was a chair maker, a miner, a blacksmith, and a farmer. The man could fix whatever you broke. But, for a claim to fame, Uncle Ed built what may be the most photographed mill in America.

Mabry Mill shows up on road maps and brochures. With more than a million visitors a year, it is possibly the most popular spot on the entire 469-mile Blue Ridge Parkway. Yet maybe Mabry should have been "Mayberry" for the same "Mayberry" where Andy and Opie went whistling down to the old fishing hole.

The Mayberry name comes from Isaac Mayberry, who secured a land grant in 1787 and gave his name to the Mayberry hamlet where Virginia's Patrick, Carroll, and Floyd counties meet. Uncle Ed is one of Isaac's descendants. So is Charles Mayberry, a son of Isaac, who shortened the family name from Mayberry to Mabry.

Mabry Mill stands about four miles north of Mayberry, Virginia, where one of actor Andy Griffith's grandfathers once regularly sold ginseng roots at the Mayberry Trading Post. As it came time to

The Mayberry Trading Post

The famous Mabry Mill on the Blue Ridge Parkway

name the TV town on "The Andy Griffith Show," the store's longtime proprietor, Coy Lee Yeatts, figured, "There was no other Mayberry around to come up with that name."

Who knows? Everyone has already figured North Carolina's Pilot Mountain morphed into TV's "Mount Pilot." Virginia's Fancy Gap made its way into "Griffith" scripts. Story lines also referenced the real-life Snappy Lunch, Wiener Burger, and Grand Theatre.

So, why not Mayberry? It's just 28 miles from Andy Griffith's hometown of Mount Airy, a lively city in North Carolina where Mayberry names are fixed on places offering haircuts, squad-car tours, Barney Fife T-shirts, pork-chop sandwiches, and all kinds of trinkets.

Unincorporated Mayberry appears much more

modest. Locals pay little mind to TV connections, and there are only a handful of landmarks noting the name, like the Mayberry Trading Post, which stands in sight of the Blue Ridge Parkway. This folksy, old store served as the now-closed Mayberry Post Office until 1922.

Just a few whistles away, the Mabrys' mom-and-pop mill survived a quarter century but then looked as tired as the Mabrys do in old photographs. Uncle Ed built the mill around 1910, pulling water from every creek, stream, and branch he could acquire. But Uncle Ed often had to wait for a wet spell, even a flood, to get his wheel turning.

Around 1930, the operation nearly ground to a halt. Ed suffered some kind of illness, losing the use of his legs. Lizzie took over. Then Ed died. Broken-hearted, Lizzie sold the mill to the National Park Service. She died in 1940.

Today, Mabry Mill looks dressed for tourists with a little log cabin designed to be the Mabrys' make-believe home. Fact is, Blue Ridge Parkway planners did not think the Mabrys' real home, a two-story frame house, looked rustic enough, so they tore it down in 1942 and moved in the log one.

The mill has since become legendary for its love-liness, even if its landscape is not historically accurate. The grounds burst with blooming flowers, and the millpond attracts ducks, dogs, and the muse of many a painter. So beautiful, so romantic, if there was ever a place to steal a kiss, surely, Mabry Mill would be it.

Blue Ridge Parkway: Mabry Mill & Mayberry Trading Post

From the Blue Ridge Passage Resort at Cockram Mill, follow US-58 west for a half mile, then turn left on US-58 Business at Meadows of Dan. Continue for one mile to the Blue Ridge Parkway entrances. Turn north on the Parkway and go 1.6 miles to Mabry Mill, on the right, at mile 176.1. A short trail leads past farm implements, a moonshine still, mill-stones, and outbuildings. Also on-site is a gift shop and short-order restaurant, open spring to fall, with a screen-porch dining room. On Sundays, musicians often play bluegrass music on the grounds.

To reach Mayberry, turn south at the Parkway entrance and go 2.6 miles to the Mayberry Trading Post, 883 Mayberry Church Rd., on the left, between mileposts 180 and 181.

Kiss of Death

It started with a kiss and ended with a killing. Five people lay dead after the trial of Floyd Allen turned into a bullet-flying bloodbath in the Carroll County Courthouse. When the smoke cleared, the dusty-street town called Hillsville would be locked in legend and loaded with lore.

Talk about a morning after. On March 15, 1912, sleepy Hillsville found its way onto the front pages of newspapers across the nation, with screaming headlines like AWFUL TRAGEDY ENACTED IN A VIRGINIA COURTHOUSE. Newspapers remained so entrenched with the story of the Allen clan that for a solid month, journalists filed dispatches about the "outlaw" Allen family on the run, until America's attention turned to the icy Atlantic and the sinking of a ship called the *Titanic*.

Talk about sensationalism. News accounts flew almost as madly as the bullets in the courthouse, whipping up stories in all directions. One tale said that store owner Floyd Allen tried to kill himself with a pocketknife. Another reported that his runaway brother, J. Sidna Allen, had been surrounded at a stop called Squirrel Spur. Yet one more account said that J. Sidna's wife was killed in a subsequent shootout.

Maybe half of the reports were accurate. The story of the post-trial gunfight at J. Sidna's house—the one when his wife was "killed"—never happened at all.

Talk about ironies. Unpretentious Hillsville has not blatantly tried to capitalize on the infamy of this incident. But courthouse tours are offered. And, in 2005, the Historical Society of Carroll County moved its library into the shooting site, where a bullet hole can still be seen on a front step of the 1872 courthouse.

On Labor Day weekends, you can also see guns carried all over Hillsville as part of the local VFW's gun show and flea market, an all-enveloping event that attracts thousands and ties up the town with turtle-speed traffic.

Back around 1910, traffic wasn't a problem. Why, there wasn't even a car in Hillsville when, as best as anyone can tell, the shootout story started at a corn shucking at nearby Fancy Gap. Nineteen-year-old Wesley Edwards found a red ear of corn, and that entitled him to kiss a girl of his choice. But, as fate would have it, the girl he kissed was already dating another young man, William Thomas.

To trace it now, that smooch would be like a kiss

of death. It would lead to a fistfight outside a church and then assault charges for Wesley Edwards and his brother, Sidna Edwards. Their uncle, Floyd Allen, stepped in, but he soon found himself under arrest for interfering with the law as deputies tried to lock up his nephews.

About a year later, Allen's long-delayed trial arrived in March 1912. And it promised to be a spectacle of intense local drama. People all over Carroll County knew that Allen—a 50-something former law officer who swore that he would never go to jail—was a tough guy. But they also knew there was a political war between the staunch Democrats of the Allen family and the Republicans who ran the county.

As many as 300 people crowded the courtroom. Many carried guns. Coming from nearby Pulaski County, Judge Thornton L. Massie didn't see much wrong with that—lots of people carried sidearms in those days.

Talk about a deadly mistake. Just seconds after Massie sentenced Allen to a year in jail, Allen replied, "I ain't a-goin'," and the shooting began. Who knows who fired first, but 57 shots blasted in 90 seconds as the flying lead spread to the courthouse lawn. Both county officers and members of the Allen family fired weapons. Massie was killed. So were Sheriff Lewis Webb, Commonwealth's Attorney William Foster, juror Augustus Fowler, and spectator Betty Ayers.

Now, talk about a great escape. Floyd Allen's gun-toting brother, J. Sidna, wound up as far away as Des Moines, Iowa, with the Allen brothers' nephew Wesley Edwards, the young man who stole the kiss and, seemingly, started it all. Finally, about six months after the shooting, detectives caught the runaways,

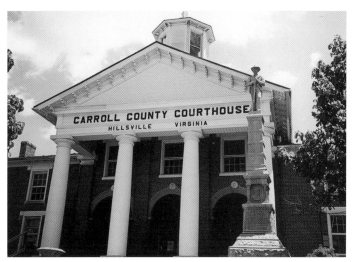

Old Carroll County Courthouse in Hillsville

and they were sentenced to lengthy jail terms. Floyd Allen and his son Claude were executed in 1913 for their roles in the shooting.

The tragedy of the day never really went away. It inspired books, songs, even a rock opera. A famous ballad, "Sidney Allen," tells a slightly fictionalized story of J. Sidna Allen and was recorded in 1924 by Henry Whitter, a guitarist and fiddler known for recording the songs "The Wreck of the Southern Old 97" as well as "New River Train."

🚗 Hillsville: Old Carroll County Courthouse

From the Blue Ridge Parkway at Meadows of Dan, follow US-58 Business west for one mile. Turn left and continue west on US-58 for 19.7 miles, passing Tory Creek (a refuge for Tories during the American Revolution), Laurel Fork (a stream named for wild laurel), and Crooked Oak (named for a bent and twisted oak tree). Turn north on US-52 (Main St.) at Hillsville and go 0.2 miles to the Old Carroll County Courthouse, 515 N. Main St., on the right.

Capital on The Crooked Road

Corwin Matthews took his guitar for a ride on the "New River Train" on a Friday night at the old Galax High School. Matthews performed the folk song as part of the first Old Fiddlers Convention, organized by the Galax Moose Lodge #733 in 1935.

The competition proved so popular, selling 300 advance tickets, that another was held later that same year. And then came another, summer after summer, until the Old Fiddlers Convention grew into one of the world's largest gatherings of traditional string artists.

Onstage, fiddlers play for prizes during the second week of August at Galax's Felts Park. Offstage, musicians informally jam in campgrounds and parking lots. It's a friendly scene. But, for a while, the frolics of the Old Fiddlers Convention seemed more like that fiddlin' sound the devil made when he went down to Georgia: rough and marred by moonshine, fights, and routine arrests.

The cleaned-up convention has since become an exit on the Crooked Road, a 253-mile driving tour through Virginia. This snake-shaped path follows US-58 and several secondary highways, linking the mountain music sites of Galax with the Blue Ridge Institute and Museum in Ferrum, Floyd Country Store in Floyd, Birthplace of Country Music Mural in Bristol, Carter Fold in Hiltons, Country Cabin in Norton, and the Ralph Stanley Museum in Clintwood.

Consider Galax the capital on the Crooked Road. It claims to be the "World's Capital of Old-Time Mountain Music." The city hosts Friday night bluegrass shows at the Rex Theater, a renovated 1939 movie house on Grayson Street. More music can be heard during the summer at Galax's Blue Ridge Music Center, just off the Blue Ridge Parkway. Some say, even, that there are more old-time fiddlers, banjo pickers, guitar players, and dulcimer strummers surrounding Galax than any other place in the world!

Galax took its name from the heart-shaped galax leaf, among the first cargo shipped from town on what became known to musicians as the "New River Train." The local railroad inspired that song, but the actual tune dates as early as 1895, years before the tracks reached Galax. The abandoned railroad line has since evolved into the New River Trail State Park, a recreation path that borders the New River for 39 of the trail's 57 miles.

🚗 Galax: New River Trail State Park & The Crooked Road

From the US-52 junction at Hillsville, follow US-58 west for 12 miles, passing the Harmon Museum, featuring local history displays, at Woodlawn (named for early settler Col. James Wood). The New River Trail State Park in Galax lies on the right at Chestnut Creek. From the red caboose, the trail goes 2.2 miles north to the park's Cliffview Ranger Station, located along VA-721.

The New River Trail stretches north to Pulaski and is open for hiking, biking, and horseback riding. Near Galax, another trail access point is located at Chestnut Yard, off VA-607, in Carroll County. Follow the trail north from this point for about one mile to get to the ten-foot-high Chestnut Creek Falls.

Near the trailhead parking lot in Galax, turn south on VA-89 to reach sites along the Crooked Road at Felts Park on Main Street and the Rex Theater, 113 Grayson St. From here, continue south on VA-89 for seven miles past Galax to find the Blue Ridge Music Center. Turn north on the Blue Ridge Parkway and go two miles to the music center entrance, near Mile 213.

The caboose at the New River Trail State Park in Galax

The New River Like It Is

If you liked the idea of building a couple of dams in Grayson County, people called you a "beaver." If you wanted to keep "The New River Like It Is," you might have been labeled an "elitist."

Such was the scene of the New River controversy, a struggle of poor farmers, politicians, and a power company. The dam plan attracted national attention, endless editorials, artistic statements, and even a radio message from Earl Hamner, Jr., creator of the television show "The Waltons." The controversy also flooded into a series of appeals and arguments that meandered through time like the river itself.

The New River had already been dammed in Virginia long before the New River controversy began in 1962. In 1903, Col. Francis Henry Fries washed Bartlett's Falls off the maps of Grayson County when he built a 39-foot-high dam to power his textile mill. The colonel's factory town of Fries—jokingly called "freeze" (the correct pronunciation) in the winter and "frize" in the summer—employed thousands over eight decades. But the Fries Dam also encouraged further ideas on how to harness the river.

Just downstream from Fries, the newly formed Appalachian Power Company constructed dams on the New River at Byllesby and Buck in 1912–1913 and, in so doing, put the site of a prosperous resort, Grayson Sulphur Springs, underwater. In 1939, the company built the much bigger Claytor Dam in Pulaski County and submerged 21 miles of riverbed, this time flooding the oldest settlement west of the New River, the circa-1744 Dunkard's Bottom.

Next came plans for the biggest dam yet: Appalachian Power's Blue Ridge Project. It would squeeze more power from the New River to generate electricity. And it would form two lakes, flooding about 20,000 acres, making the flat water above the Fries Dam look like a backyard pond.

The New River gets its start in North Carolina's High Country. It waddles across the Virginia–North Carolina border, zigzagging for a few miles, before finally setting its backward course, uniquely running south to north and then west. Downstream of Claytor Dam, the river wraps around Radford University, fumbles over the falls of McCoy, and finally joins the Gauley River to form the Kanawha River in West Virginia.

Appalachian Power planned to cage the river right

The New River at Baywood

above that Virginia-Carolina zigzag by building two dams in southern Grayson County. By 1968, however, the initial plan doubled, taking a suggestion by the Department of the Interior, which wanted the waters of the New to flush out the industrial wastes of West Virginia that lay downstream.

This bigger plan would flood about 26,000 acres in Grayson County and about 14,000 acres in North Carolina, mostly in Ashe County. The sheer size of the two lakes would nearly rival the twin-lake scene of Lake Gaston and Buggs Island Lake, also on the Virginia–North Carolina border. The New River lakes also promised the same big-time recreation and development, with marinas, beaches, dozens of islands, a state park in Virginia, and another in North Carolina.

Many politicians liked the idea of opening the sparsely populated Appalachian Mountains to this opportunity. Many "beavers" saw riches in building the dams and later collecting the big bucks tourists would leave behind.

Many others opposed the great walls of water. These lakes would destroy 200-year-old farms and displace nearly 3,000 people. In Grayson County, the water would completely swallow Mouth of Wilson and bury a big part of Baywood. It would flood forever about 44 miles of the main river channel, more than twice the length of Claytor Lake.

There were court cases. There were debates. More than 100 newspapers turned in editorials against the project, and Hamner was heard on radio stations, saying, "Please think twice before you destroy the New River."

In Ashe County, about 3,000 people against the project gathered at the Festival for the New River on July 26, 1975. This event celebrated the river's beauty and history, with singers and artists performing for the attendants. But it might have also seemed like a funeral. By then, the Federal Power Commission had already issued a license to build the dams, and much land had been acquired for the flood zone.

Some landowners refused to sell. They vowed to fight forever; they wore their anti-dam slogan, "New River Like It Is," on T-shirts and displayed it on their cars with bumper stickers. In turn, the power company launched a national advertising campaign to promote the dam, calling its opponents "elitists." But many of these opponents simply were farming families who had lived along the river for generations, and, not knowing when the lake would be built, they had put their lives on hold.

As it turned out, the lake was never built. In 1976, Congress passed a bill that designated a 26.5-mile section of the New River in North Carolina a National Wild and Scenic River. This action essentially revoked the company's license to build the dams in Grayson County. President Gerald Ford signed the bill into law on September 11, 1976, and one of the strongest opponents of the dams, North Carolina Gov. James E. Holshouser, presented a certificate naming Ford an "Admiral of the New River Navy."

An old-age claim helped persuade politicians to save the New River. Scientists had said the New River was actually the "Old River," predating the surrounding Appalachian Mountains, and that's why it flows backward. The "New" moniker likely came from the way mapmakers once called Virginia the "New World," and what lay beyond the Blue Ridge Mountains, including this river, was called "New Virginia."

Today, the New River retains its curvy figure along its Carolina-Virginia zigzag. Still wild and scenic, its waters slide and fall, meandering through time.

🚗 Baywood: New River

From the New River Trail State Park at VA-89 in Galax, continue west on US-58 for eight miles to the New River bridge and public river access at Baywood, on the right. This area would have been flooded under plans of the Blue Ridge Project.

A float downstream from Baywood leads eight miles to a public landing at Riverside, with a journey through Class I-II rapids. The Riverside takeout lies off VA-274, about 7.5 miles north of US-58.

Powerhouse Falls

Powerhouse Falls

Even when it was privately owned, folks still made treks to Peach Bottom Falls at Independence. Maybe that was trespassing. But the landowner simply let people go swim and slide anyway. As with any good waterfall, property owners couldn't keep the curious away. So in 2004, the Grayson County Board of Supervisors bought the beautiful collection of cascades and established a public park.

Size-wise, with a total drop of 100 feet, Peach Bottom ranks somewhere in the middle of Virginia's hundreds of waterfalls. The highest and most well-known plunge may be Nelson County's Crabtree Falls, with a drop of over 1,000 feet.

Yet Peach Bottom is known for more than its beauty or its size. In the 1780s, Matthew Dickey operated Point Hope Furnace at this natural landmark. Dickey harnessed the waterfall's power, forged tools from locally mined iron ore, and shipped his wares west on the Holston River, far beyond Independence.

Peach Bottom Falls briefly became "Powerhouse Falls" in the early 1900s. Garnett Davis used the waterfall to turn a mill at his wooden powerhouse. That mill, in turn, supplied electrical power for a few hours a day to the people of Independence.

Peach Bottom or "Powerhouse" Falls in Grayson County

The Independence name remembers an independent group of citizens who refused to take sides during a fight to move the county courthouse. Ultimately, the courthouse moved to this group's neighborhood. Thomas Jefferson would love it—the local newspaper is called the *Declaration* (of Independence). And one of the town's biggest parties of the year happens on the Fourth of July.

🚗 *Independence: Peach Bottom Falls & 1908 Grayson County Courthouse*

From the New River bridge at Baywood, continue west on US-58 for 5.5 miles to Rt. 1124 at Independence. Turn right and go a half mile, then turn right on VA-685 (Powerhouse Rd.) and go 0.9 miles to Peach Bottom Falls, on the left. A short trail leads to the waterfall. The powerhouse no longer stands, but stone foundations of the mill remain attached to the creek's rocky slopes. From here, retrace the route to US-58. Turn right and go 0.9 miles to the 1908 Grayson County Courthouse, 107 E. Main St., at US-21. This brick landmark contains a museum with exhibits of local history, a gift shop, and an auditorium that often features live bluegrass music.

Mount Rogers Ponies

In 1976, the president of the Wilburn Ridge Pony Association made a prediction to a local newspaper, saying sales of a small herd of feral ponies living near Mount Rogers would one day "put Chincoteague Island and its pony auction off the map."

Whoa! Talk about an aspiration—Chincoteague Island's famous pony auction dates back to 1925. Each year, thousands show up not just to bid but to watch about 150 wild ponies swim from the marshy forest of Assateague Island to suburban Chincoteague Island on Virginia's Eastern Shore.

The rock-hopping horses of Virginia's High Country, however, live in an inverse environment. At elevations reaching 5,000 feet, about 125 Mount Rogers ponies tromp among the topsy-turvy terrain of Wilburn Ridge, where rocks form stairways to heavenly views.

It snows often in this windblown portion of Grayson County. But the Mount Rogers ponies possess thick and beautiful manes—woolly like a bear's, flopping over their faces—practically perfect for withstanding winters of subfreezing temperatures. Still, these playful ponies look for warmth where they can

find it, sometimes turning the area's Appalachian Trail shelters into stables.

About 25 Shetland ponies arrived in the Mount Rogers National Recreation Area in 1974 to clear brush from the area's balds. Prior to the ponies, Forest Service officials had trotted out similar experiments with other animals. But the winters turned too harsh for cattle, too cold for goats, and too barren for sheep—they munched on mountain laurel instead of spring grass and dropped dead.

Yet the ponies have thrived on Mount Rogers. They have done so well that excess numbers, like the Chincoteague ponies, are auctioned annually to keep herd numbers low. Park officials round up wild-running mares and stallions from behind rocks and brush for an annual health inspection. Then, though the event is not as famous as the Chincoteague auction, a few yearlings are sold each September during the fall festival at Grayson Highlands State Park.

Some environmentalists, meanwhile, have complained about the presence of the ponies, saying the animals might be invasive to the Mount Rogers area's fragile subalpine environment. The ponies, in turn, are locked out of certain places, including the Lewis

Wild ponies at Wilburn Ridge in Grayson County

ing through Mouth of Wilson (named for the mouth of Wilson Creek) and Volney (named for Volney Hash, whose father helped establish the local post office) as US-58 threads its way through a curvy crunch-zone of inclines. Turn right at the Grayson Highlands State Park entrance on VA-362 and follow the park road to the Massie Gap parking area.

Trails from Massie Gap lead to the Mount Rogers ponies by following the Rhododendron Trail for about two miles to Wilburn Ridge. You can also follow the park road to the campground, where ponies sometimes stand in fields along the road. The 4,935-acre state park features a playground, a picnic area, and a visitor center with trail maps. The park's 1.9-mile Cabin Creek Trail passes a 25-foot-high waterfall, while the 1.8-mile Wilson Creek Trail slides past several cascades.

Fork Wilderness Area, home of the actual summit of mile-high Mount Rogers.

🚗 *Grayson County: Grayson Highlands State Park*
From US-21 at the 1908 Grayson County Courthouse, continue west for 24.5 miles, pass-

Virginia's Rooftop

Curtains of moss hang heavy on nearly everything atop Mount Rogers, except for one well-known rock planted at the top, a God-given point for picnics. Looking up, the clouds are so close that it feels like only a short hop to Heaven.

Elevation: 5,729 feet above sea level.

This is Virginia's rooftop, an isolated island in the sky where fog rolls in on a whim and five feet of rain falls each year. Mount Rogers holds the claim of the tallest spot in Virginia, with Canadian-style woods supporting a sanctuary of ferns, firs, and wood sorrel. An intricate plant, the wood sorrel appears similar to a shamrock and makes mystical Mount Rogers look like a land where leprechauns live.

How appropriate. Often, early settlers compared high, lonesome lands like this to their ancestral homes of Ireland, Scotland, and Germany. These transplanted Europeans brought time-honored traditions of religion, food, and song to the Virginia Highlands. And their fiddle tunes blended beautifully with the shrill of songbirds and babbling brooks, the natural music of the mountains.

Such mountain music inspired Albert Hash for 55 years. And, through his legacy, that inspiration continues. A grandson of a medicine-show fiddler, and a descendant of early settlers, Hash was born near the foot of Mount Rogers in 1917. He played fiddle, made fiddles, and taught his craft to many Mount Rogers musicians, including world-renowned guitarist and guitar-maker Wayne Henderson. Just a year before he died, the affable Hash expanded his music

The arched entrance to the Mount Rogers School

lessons in 1982 to his alma mater, the tiny Mount Rogers School in Grayson County.

Both handsome and charming, built from stones in the 1930s, the Mount Rogers School welcomes kindergartners to high school seniors. Inside, student members of the Albert Hash Memorial Band strum banjos, dulcimers, and guitars, while faraway suburban schools blow saxophones, trombones, and trumpets. Here, a violin is called a fiddle. And the band repertoire, like picking "Wildwood Flower," overlaps with family tradition. Students here say they have no interest in a horn-blowing band—mountain music suits them just fine.

Mount Rogers School and the summit of Mount Rogers are named for William Barton Rogers, the state's first geologist. In 1835, Rogers began an exhaustive geologic survey of Virginia. His crew's ambition, however, went unfulfilled—the Virginia General Assembly cut funding for the study in 1842. Rogers later founded the Massachusetts Institute of Technology. In 1882, he collapsed in mid-speech while delivering that school's commencement address. He said his final words—"bituminous coal"—and died at the podium.

Earlier, Mount Rogers was called "Balsam Mountain" for its native balsams, trees now referred to as Fraser firs. The peak marks the northernmost natural range of the species.

Mossy forest atop Mount Rogers

The Appalachian Trail rings the mountain, but thru-hikers often bypass the half-mile spur leading atop, saying they've heard there is no view. Truly, there is none, at least in the way of seeing far into a valley. But in the early 1970s, thru-hikers had no choice. The AT ran right across the top of the peak.

In 1975, longtime trail volunteers David and Nerine Thomas rerouted the hiking path following a Forest Service request to protect the mountain's rare plants from being trampled.

Later, in 1991, David Thomas became a Mount Rogers legend for trucking logs by bulldozer along the Lewis Fork, four miles from any road. His volunteer crew built an Appalachian Trail shelter, and quick. Thomas said, "The day we finished that shelter, they were lined up there to spend the night—a group of boy scouts. There were 25 waiting for us to nail down the floor."

To Thomas's surprise, Mount Rogers National Recreation Area officials later named the hut "Thomas Knob Shelter." It sits about one mile above sea level, less than a mile down the trail from the summit of Mount Rogers.

🚗 Grayson/Smyth counties: Mount Rogers & Mount Rogers School

The actual summit of Mount Rogers can be reached by a moderate hike from Massie Gap at Grayson Highlands State Park. Follow the park's Rhododendron Trail to the Appalachian Trail, reaching Wilburn Ridge in about two miles, and go another two miles (passing through a rock passage called the "Fat-Man Squeeze Tunnel") to a sign marking the half-mile Mount Rogers spur, just beyond the Thomas Knob Shelter.

You can also reach Mount Rogers from Elk Garden. To get there from Grayson Highlands State Park, follow US-58 west for 3.7 miles to Mount Rogers School, on the left, then continue on US-58 for another 3.9 miles (7.6 miles west of Grayson Highlands State Park). Turn right on VA-600 at the Whitetop Post Office. Go 2.7 miles north to Elk Garden at the Appalachian Trail parking lot. From here, follow the Appalachian Trail north for four miles to the Mount Rogers spur.

The Appalachian Trail is marked by vertical, two-by-six-inch white paint blazes. A double blaze—one above the other—is placed before turns or junctions.

Eleanor Was Here

When Eleanor Roosevelt walked atop Whitetop Mountain on August 12, 1933, as many as 20,000 people turned out to see her. It was the most celebrated moment during all of the Whitetop Folk Festivals in the 1930s. And, as a way to roll out the red carpet, the road ascending the 5,520-foot-high peak was widened so the First Lady could arrive in a luxury sedan.

The Whitetop Folk Festival had been going on for a couple of years as a contest of old-time mountain musicians, overseen by Abingdon attorney John Blakemore, Annabel Morris Buchanan of nearby Marion, and John Powell, a classical composer. Each August, players vied for $10 prizes, a precious reward during the Great Depression.

Their stage could not have been more grand: a dance hall and big rows of tents stood on the grassy carpet of Whitetop's prairie, a field that looks white at a distance. This mountaintop bald might have been caused by Cherokees burning off trees to attract deer to an open area. A legend says the Cherokee once used this space for signal fires.

Eleanor Roosevelt considered Whitetop Mountain and the nearby community of Abingdon part of the puzzle of her youth. This is where her father, Elliott Roosevelt, spent two years of his life and communicated with his long-distance daughter through a series of letters, calling her "Little Nell."

A handsome hunter and sportsman, Elliott Roosevelt had shown up in Abingdon in 1892. Warm, inviting, and everywhere the life of the party, Roosevelt said he came to the Virginia Highlands to look after the Whitetop Mountain timber interests owned by his sister Corinne and her husband, Douglas Robinson. Roosevelt also sought renewed health from shattered nerves.

The truth was, the other well-heeled Roosevelts of New York had exiled Elliott for his drinking. Often, he had turned violent and mortified his wife and Eleanor's mother, Anna, who said she didn't want him back until he had proven his sobriety. So off he went to Virginia, away from his wife, away from Little Nell, and away from the political spotlight that shined ever so brightly on his brother—and future president—Teddy Roosevelt.

On the hunt, Elliott Roosevelt rounded the Virginia hills with his dogs and horses; sometimes he stopped at farms, asking for pitchers of buttermilk.

Odd outcrops stand in the prairie of Whitetop Mountain

Roosevelt rewarded five-dollar pieces to whoever quenched his thirst. He also rewarded hungry families at Christmas, distributing hundreds of turkeys that he had bought from local farmers.

Roosevelt, too, enjoyed horseplay. During one particularly snowy winter, he rallied in the streets of Abingdon for everyone young and old to come out and go sledding. He even ripped down fences for people to use sleds.

But Roosevelt's life took a real slide. His wife, Anna, died of diphtheria at age 29. His namesake son, Elliott Jr., died a few months later. By the summer of 1894, Roosevelt had moved back to New York. He was drinking again. Then in August, he was dead at age 34 after falling down a flight of stairs. Little Nell was only ten.

Growing up an orphan, Eleanor Roosevelt always wondered about the years she missed with her father. In 1915, she married a distant cousin, Franklin Delano Roosevelt, and in 1932 she found herself in the White House. The following spring, Eleanor contacted Buchanan and made arrangements to attend the Whitetop Folk Festival.

Little Nell wanted to see her father's old stomping grounds and meet some of his old friends.

Her train from Washington, D.C., arrived in Abingdon at 10:00 A.M., greeting a large crowd. Mayor Ray B. Hagy delivered a speech and was probably nervous, using notes he had placed inside his straw hat. Washington County Sheriff Keys Boardwine then led the long charge uphill to Whitetop, driving Eleanor in a borrowed Lincoln for more than 35 miles.

Musicians atop the mountain met the First Lady with mutual admiration. They sang "Happy Days Are Here Again," and she smiled. "To the people who live here," Eleanor told the crowd, "I want to say a special word of gratitude. They have given me the feeling that they remember affectionately my father, whom I adore."

Eleanor ate fried chicken and Virginia ham. And she was framed by a swarm of cameramen, including one newspaper photographer from Washington, D.C., who ventured too far on an overhanging ledge to get a better shot. "He slipped and fell," John Blakemore told a newspaper years later, "but by grabbing a tree limb saved himself from crashing into a 200-foot abutment."

By the afternoon, the First Lady left the mountain with flowers and gifts. Just before nightfall, she boarded the train at Abingdon and was whisked away to Washington. The original Whitetop Folk Festival continued for a few more years after Eleanor was here but never past 1940, when heavy rains temporarily washed out the road ascending the peak.

Now Whitetop Mountain slumbers in silence, draped in winter with blankets of ice and snow. The old Whitetop Dance Hall used during the festivals has since been torn down; parts were salvaged to build the nearby Mount Rogers Fire Hall. But, in August, you can walk Whitetop's ageless bald, find wildflowers, and soak up its vast and gorgeous view—warm and inviting, just like that day when Eleanor was here.

🚗 Whitetop: Whitetop Mountain

From Mount Rogers School at VA-751, follow US-58 for 3.9 miles to the Whitetop Post Office. Turn right on VA-600 and go north for 1.5 miles. Turn left on USFS-89 and go 3 miles to reach the top of the mountain.

Whitetop's gravel forest road makes wide-swinging switchbacks in the meadow atop the mountain. Here, the Appalachian Trail crosses the road. Following the trail south from this point leads one mile downhill to Buzzard Rock, an outcrop that overlooks North Carolina, Virginia, and Tennessee.

Creeper Country

Creeper Country

Winston Link loved steamy sights, especially a puffy plume curling into clouds above a steam locomotive. But, in the late 1950s, the New York photographer had to race against time to lasso such snorting iron horses. Steam trains were slated for extinction on the Norfolk & Western Railway; they would soon be replaced by diesel engines.

So Link packed cameras in his convertible and captured all he could. He wandered beside an old logging line, the Abingdon Branch of the Norfolk & Western Railway, and shot one of his most famous frames, "Old Maud Bows to the Virginia Creeper," at the Green Cove Depot.

Standing since 1914, the Green Cove Depot was built when the Abingdon Branch was still called the Virginia-Carolina Railway. Thousands of men once cut wood along its attached arms of narrow gauge lines, reaching far into ancient Appalachian forests of poplar and chestnut. In the early 1900s, this mountain scene was like a gold rush, and a few prospectors raped the ridges for any virgin timber an ax could find. Some left entire mountainsides barren, studded by stumps and worth no more than practically acorns on the acre.

After 24 years, operations in the lumber town of Konnarock sawed out on Christmas Eve 1928. Large-scale logging was over, and much of the surrounding land later became part of a national forest, with hopes that, someday, riches would return.

With or without a load of logs, trains slowly kept chugging on the steep grades of the railroad, rumbling over trestles and rambling past campsites used by Daniel Boone in the 1700s. At its height, the line spanned 76 miles, linking Abingdon, Virginia, to Elkland, North Carolina.

In between stood Green Cove, the place where Link shot "Old Maud Bows to the Virginia Creeper" in 1956. This photo artistically states the passing of two endangered eras with a scene of a big white horse bowing to the snort of a steam locomotive. Recalling in 1995 that he "had this horse set up," Link said that his railroad photographs worked well, generally, because he carefully placed props with the cooperation of train officials. In this case, the horse named "Old Maud" belonged to a local family and probably acted naturally; it's been said that she had a habit of holding her head down in a bowing position.

The Green Cove Depot belonged to William M.

The Virginia Creeper Trail links Abingdon to Whitetop.

Buchanan, a schoolteacher-turned-station-manager known best as "Mr. Buck." Buchanan bought the wooden one-story and thereby saved it from destruction when all trains—even the diesel engines—stopped running on the Abingdon Branch on March 31, 1977.

Ten years later, a 34-mile section of the landmark line became the Virginia Creeper Trail with major stops at Abingdon, Damascus, Green Cove, and Whitetop. The path uses the nickname for the Virginia-Carolina Railway. Some say "Virginia Creeper" comes from the steam trains slowly creeping uphill. Others swear it stems from the Virginia creeper vines lining lush jungles, sprawling over once-naked slopes in the national forest.

Casual cyclists coast through the rich woods of the Creeper country, following downhill from a life-size replica of the original Whitetop Station to the Green Cove Depot. Diehard cyclists, like Lawrence Dye, make tracks both ways, even the uphill trudge.

In 2005, the 73-year-old Dye became a legend on the Virginia Creeper Trail after registering 100,000 miles of round-trips, relentlessly cycling in sunshine or snow. Once a schoolteacher like William M. Buchanan, he loved Green Cove just like Link loved trains. And he became predictable like a train. Dye made daily stops at the Green Cove Depot, always refueling himself with peanut butter and apple butter on a triple-stack sandwich. Then, bowing his head like Old Maud, he would pedal back down that rail-to-trail road to Damascus.

Green Cove Depot

🚗 Green Cove: Virginia Creeper Trail

From Whitetop to Damascus, US-58 rolls through the scenic Mount Rogers National Recreation Area like a roller coaster, twisting and turning but nearly always keeping the Virginia Creeper Trail in sight. To reach the Whitetop Station from the Whitetop Post Office at VA-600, follow US-58 for one mile to a left turn at VA-754 and go two miles to the station, on the left, at VA-726. Then return to US-58, turn left, and go west for 2.5 miles. Turn left on VA-600 and go 0.4 miles to Green Cove Depot. Then return again to US-58, turn left, and go west for 5.2 miles to the Virginia Creeper Trail's Creek Junction Area, on the left, with handicapped-accessible fishing piers on Whitetop Laurel Creek.

Beyond Creek Junction, go another six miles west on US-58, passing Beartree Recreation Area (with a campground, fishing lake, and swimming beach) and the roadside waterfalls of the Straight Branch to reach the Virginia Creeper Trail's Straight Branch parking lot, on the left. From here, US-58 runs west for 4.6 miles to the Damascus Community Park, where the Virginia Creeper Trail intersects the Appalachian Trail. The Creeper Trail continues for 17 miles west of Damascus to Abingdon.

Virginia Creeper Trail access points are also located at the junction of VA-725 and VA-726 in Taylors Valley; near the Holston River bridge on VA-710 at Alvarado; along VA-677 at Watauga; and at the corner of A Street and Green Springs Road in Abingdon.

Holy Ground for Hikers

From all over the world, people make tracks through Damascus not by bus, but by boot. These Appalachian Trail hikers start south at Springer Mountain, Georgia, and they will have walked hundreds of miles before reaching Damascus, where the world's longest continually marked footpath turns from moss to mortar, marching up Laurel Avenue on a brick sidewalk.

There are no age limits. Some hikers are college kids calling themselves names like "Gypsy," and they'll tackle the 2,167-mile-long trail while looking for themselves, or maybe their next college major. Some are restless retirees, like the 65-year-old mechanic who strapped on an outdated backpack and dubbed himself "65 and Alive."

Southern thru-hikers call this the "Ap-pa-latch-un Trail," while Northerners say "Ap-pa-lay-shun." By many accounts, "Appalachian" is derived from the Appalachee Indian tribe discovered by the Spanish in the 1500s.

The Appalachian Trail grew from the dreams of Benton MacKaye, a forester who,

in the 1920s, envisioned a footpath tracing the ridge crests of the Appalachian Mountains from Georgia to Maine.

Damascus adopted its Biblical name in 1886, when Courtland, Virginia, was still called "Jerusalem." Confederate Brig. Gen. John D. Imboden named Damascus, and he figured he would get rich from all the iron inside nearby Iron Mountain. Imboden

Appalachian Trail in Damascus

formed the Damascus Enterprise Company with several partners, including brothers A. D. Reynolds and R. J. Reynolds of Patrick County. But, as it turned out, Iron Mountain was not so aptly named, because the iron deposits were not enough to start a steel industry. Still, Imboden liked Damascus, and he spent his final years in town selling bottled springwater in the 1890s.

The town's Biblical name still fits. Damascus is holy ground for hikers, especially during Appalachian Trail Days in May, when thousands gather for what looks like a backwoods Mardi Gras. A tent city blossoms on the banks of Laurel Creek, and dozens crowd into the Place, a hostel that took its name from an unknown hiker who carved "This is the place" on some wood and left the sign at the hostel's back door.

Trail Days can grow crazy, especially during the Hiker Parade. This casual march down Laurel Avenue features a hodgepodge of colorful costumes, just like Mardi Gras. Hikers playfully shoot squirt guns and toss water balloons. Still, that flying water could be considered a baptism in the thru-hiking lifestyle: walk a week with no bath, never shave, and sleep in trail shelters from Georgia to Maine.

Damascus: Appalachian Trail

The Appalachian Trail intersects US-58 and runs down the sidewalks of Laurel Avenue to Damascus Community Park at the corner of West Laurel Avenue (US-58) and South Beaverdam Avenue. The park includes a gazebo, a playground, and a railroad caboose, where Forest Service officials distribute brochures on the Appalachian Trail and Mount Rogers National Recreation Area. The Place, 203 E. Bank Ave., stands behind the Damascus United Methodist Church, about a block off US-58.

Southwest

Scenic valleys boast vibrant villages in Southwest Virginia, from artsy Abingdon to the state-line-straddling city of Bristol. Actor Mel Gibson once walked the small-town streets of Gate City to film a movie called *The River.* Farther west, Jonesville marks the birthplace of Dr. Andrew Taylor Still, the father of osteopathic medicine.

Here also is the land where Daniel Boone marked a road west—beyond Wheeler and Gibson Station—to reach Kentucky's bluegrass through the Cumberland Gap.

Play Something, Beth

Bill Clinton and Jimmy Carter have checked in. So has Elizabeth Taylor. But the name that has won more fame than any other at the lavish Martha Washington Inn in Abingdon, Virginia, is not on the guest register. It is "Beth," the name of the college girl who haunts the four-star hotel on full-moon nights with her mysterious violin music.

Over several years, hotel guests and employees have reported feeling touched by spirits. And some have claimed to see the floating figure of a girl, often called "Beth," wearing what longtime hotel employee Pete Sheffey dubbed "an apron-type dress and high-buckle shoes."

There's also a story told about a mysterious Civil War soldier hobbling down a hallway with a bloody leg or missing limb. Dates of this account have varied, but the ghostly soldier was reportedly seen by a policeman and left bloody marks on a floor before disappearing outside.

Conversely, some employees have worked at the Martha Washington Inn for years without even the most remote haunting encounter.

Blame the beginning, perhaps, on the "Martha Girls," the students of the Martha Washington College. For more than 80 years, from the Civil War until the Great Depression, this school occupied the hotel buildings. The all-girl college students followed rigid rules that, likely, sparked great imaginations.

Boys from nearby Emory & Henry College could write notes to the Martha Girls, but the girls could reply only with the permission of the college president. The girls were not allowed to drink cherry Cokes, nor could they wave at train conductors. And if they smoked, they got expelled.

Before it was a college, the central portion of the hotel was the family home of the wealthy Gen. Francis Preston, who grew up at the Smithfield Plantation of Blacksburg, Virginia, and made a fortune mining salt in nearby Saltville. As a 27-year-old attorney, Preston took a 14-year-old girl, Sarah Campbell, to be his bride in 1793. She came from good stock; her uncle was Patrick Henry, and her father was the late Gen. William Campbell, who led the Overmountain Men to an American victory over the British at the Battle of King's Mountain in 1780.

Martha Washington College opened in 1860 inside the circa-1832 Preston mansion. Four years later, the first class graduated. That same year, Union troops marched through Abingdon and burned buildings during the Civil War.

About this time comes the story of Beth, a student nurse when the college became a wartime hospital. Beth cared for a wounded Union spy in Room No. 60 (now Room 403), but the man's condition only got worse. In his last breaths, he called out, "Play something, Beth. I'm going." And she played her violin.

Today, some say, she is still playing that same melody as a musical ghost on the hotel's third floor!

Sheffey, for one, has heard mysterious music in the hotel. But a guest who made a similar claim listened to a comic surprise—hotel employees discovered this guest had been lodged next door to a concert violinist scheduled to play later that evening at Emory & Henry College.

The Martha Washington Inn in Abingdon

🚗 Abingdon: Martha Washington Inn

From the Damascus Community Park, follow US-58 west for 10.5 miles, crossing two forks of the Holston River (a watercourse named for Stephen Holstein, who took a canoe down its path in 1749). Reaching Abingdon, US-58 overlaps I-81. Follow south for two miles to Exit 17. Turn right on Cummings Street, go one mile, and turn right on US-11 to reach the Martha Washington Inn at 150 W. Main St.

The hotel sits at the center of Abingdon, a small town known for its art galleries, museums, and gift shops. Incorporated in 1778, Abingdon most likely takes its name from early settlers wanting to honor Martha Washington's ancestral home, England's Abingdon Parish.

If You Like Us, Talk About Us

Robert Porterfield provided miracles on Main Street. He made Gregory Peck funny. He turned Ernest Borgnine into more than a truck driver. He also never stopped smiling when he told his Barter Theatre audiences, "If you like us, talk about us. If you don't, just keep your mouth shut."

Born in 1905 at Austinville, Virginia, Porterfield grew up in Saltville, a few miles northwest of Abingdon. Porterfield dreamed, at age ten, that he would become an actor. By the late 1920s, he was doing just that in New York. Then out of work during the Great Depression, he chose a change of scenery.

He came home to Virginia but stopped in Abingdon, tagging along a rag-tag bunch, hitchhiking into town. These 22 out-of-work actors were wild and hairy, especially unkempt for 1933, and certainly not a hand-in-glove fit with the white-gloved ladies of the genteel town. Why, some of the women in Porterfield's bunch even smoked!

But the clean-cut Porterfield could charm anyone, and he built a bridge in this small-town society by hauling his actors into an Abingdon church and showing how well they could sing "Rock of Ages."

Next, Porterfield got down to business. He announced that his transplanted troupe would be staging shows in Abingdon, and to get in, you could pay 35 cents or trade some victuals.

Call that crazy, but not here. Bartering had been a rule in Abingdon since the frontier times of the 1700s. And Porterfield's new Barter Theatre found farmers gladly forking over veggies to see a musical or comedy.

Barter's opening night on June 10, 1933, was hog wild. Somebody traded a pig to get in the door, and it was tied up outside, squealing like a barker.

Another time, a ticket-taker squealed as a man tried to slip her a dead rattlesnake. The man promised, "Rattlers is good vittles."

Then came the guy with the cow. He milked it on Main Street but presented only enough milk to pay his own way. The ticket-taker asked the man about his wife's admission, to which the man replied, "Let 'er milk 'er own ticket."

And it went on like that, night after night. Turtles got loose in the lobby. A pig got loose on the street. One man handed over a calf but wouldn't give up its rope. The calf got loose in the theater, and showtime was delayed for five minutes.

Barter Theatre in Abingdon

About 90 percent of theater patrons traded their way into shows with garden bounties. Some earmarked ears of corn for admission. Some planted an extra row of beans for barter.

A local sheriff also helped the theater's 1930s production of *Mountain Ivy* when he staged a raid on nearby Whitetop Mountain and provided a moonshine still for the set. Still, there was a problem with the law, namely the town jail. It was located in the basement of Barter Theatre's circa-1830 building on Main Street. Actors shared this brick landmark in the 1930s. Yet the inmates in the basement jail were at times so noisy that it was hard to hear the actors on the Barter Theatre stage.

But the crowds kept coming, and the theater's reputation grew, like the actors' waistlines and the Barter Theatre's roster of stars.

In 1940, young Gregory Peck nabbed his first professional acting job at Barter Theatre. Yet Peck acted so serious that Porterfield made him practice loosening up. Peck was assigned to visit Porterfield's office each day and tell a funny anecdote. That exercise eventually relaxed Peck's nervous tension. The actor went on to star in acclaimed movies, playing attorney Atticus Finch in *To Kill a Mockingbird* and Gen. Douglas MacArthur in *MacArthur*.

During World War II, the real-life MacArthur took center stage in the Pacific Theater, while the Barter Theatre stage went dark. After the war, cash became common to pay for admission when the Barter Theatre reopened in 1946. Two years later, a 1948 show called *Papa Is All* featured young Ernest Borgnine, who first worked at the theater as a stagehand and truck driver. Porterfield discovered that Borgnine could act. Later, Borgnine starred in movies and TV's *McHale's Navy*.

Porterfield died in 1971, but the show went on at the Barter Theatre. Some say, too, that he never really left the building. Actors claim the jovial founder has reappeared as a friendly ghost, overseeing all.

But who knows what Porterfield would have thought of *Liquid Moon,* the most talked about stage show of 2003. This play, starring Elizabeth McKnight and Michael Poisson, won sensational headlines for its full-frontal nudity inside what was once a church, a playhouse on Main Street called Barter Stage II. Critics praised the thought-provoking dialogue of *Liquid Moon.* Clergy complained about the controversial content. And Richard Rose, the theater's artistic director, repeated Porterfield's immortal opening line: "If you like us, talk about us. If you don't, just keep your mouth shut."

🚗 *Abingdon: Barter Theatre*

Barter Theatre, 133 W. Main St., stands across from the Martha Washington Inn. Barter Stage II stands immediately north of the inn at Main Street's intersection with South Church Street. From here, retrace Main Street to Cummings Street. Turn left and go one mile to US-58 (I-81) at Exit 17.

At the Moonlite

illiam Booker found himself in the spotlight of the Moonlite Theatre after trying to sneak through the gate without paying. Owner Walter Mays caught the 12-year-old crouching in the backseat of a car, but cut him a deal. Mays told Booker to pick up trash around the drive-in movie theater for four weeks.

That was 1970. By 1992, Mays was retired and Booker owned the drive-in—he had fallen in love with all the nostalgia attached to the landmark Moonlite Theatre, where stars can be seen on both sides of the screen.

Built by T. D. Fields, the Moonlite opened on June 9, 1949, showing *Down to Earth,* starring Rita Hayworth and Larry Parks. In the late 1950s, the Moonlite was one of more than 4,000 drive-ins in the United States. By 2006, little more than 400 remained in operation, less than a dozen in Virginia.

The roadside marquee of the Moonlite Theatre in Abingdon

Mays once charged cable television with the demise of drive-ins. But rising real estate values could be the ticket. In growing suburbs, the acreage needed for a drive-in theater might be more profitable if the land were simply spliced and reedited as a scene for condominiums.

Still, the Moonlite successfully reels in the years. Summer after summer, the focus is retro. Teenagers pull up the hill to the make-out row. And the Moonlite sign lights up a show of neon stars while, opposite, flicks flicker on the 67-foot-tall screen.

In music, the Moonlite has been memorialized, with Rafe Van Hoy singing "At the Moonlite." And a bluegrass band, the Blinky Moon Boys, named an entire album for the theater. Booker and the Moonlite staff, meanwhile, have affectionately memorialized Mays, saying the late theater owner could be moonlighting at the Moonlite in spirit.

🚗 *Abingdon: Moonlite Theatre*

From I-81 Exit 17, go south on I-81 (US-58) for four miles to I-81 Exit 13. Turn right at the ramp and go 0.1 miles on Spring Creek Road to the Lee Highway intersection. Turn left on US-11/19 and go a half mile south to the Moonlite Theatre, on the right. Next door stands Dixie Pottery, open since

Moonlite Theatre was named a state historic landmark in 2007.

1957, selling baskets, candles, and glassware. From here, retrace the route to I-81 Exit 13.

Fake Lake

Topographic maps say all this is supposed to be underwater: the ducks and the geese that splash into the shallow ponds, and the fox sedge sprouting in the swampy sanctuary. These are the Sugar Hollow wetlands, burrowed along Beaver Creek. Contour maps paint all of this blue, calling it "Beaver Creek Lake," immediately upstream from Beaver Creek Dam.

Walking the wetlands trail in the "Fake Lake" of Bristol

Those maps are wrong. Beaver Creek Lake is a fake. It's actually only a retention basin, a fort against flooding, guarded by an 85-foot-high dam that looks like the natural hills of Bristol.

The dam forms the grassy centerpiece of Bristol's 400-acre Sugar Hollow Park. In 1965, the Tennessee Valley Authority built the dam on land once belonging to the family of Margaret Brown Preston, the youngest sister of Gen. Francis Preston, the original owner of what is now Abingdon's Martha Washington Inn. Margaret Preston married a cousin, Col. John Preston, and lived part of the 19th century at Preston's Grove, a brick house standing on the northern edge of Sugar Hollow Park.

Low-lying land above the dam grows soggy in spring. Sometimes, when it rains, it looks like it has gone coastal. More than once, park personnel have fished picnic tables out of trees and lost lawn mowers in mud.

But they really had to work after 2002, when Bristol city leaders failed to meet a deadline to install a gas-extraction system at an old landfill a few miles from the park. Virginia's environmental regulators called foul on the failure but provided a choice for punishment: pay a fine, or create a project in the city to enhance the local environment.

As it turned out, workers at Sugar Hollow Park would rake muck for months, building a bog, producing ponds, and firming up a footbridge to stretch 700 feet above mud-crusted flats. This project made up for the mess at the landfill and created the Sugar Hollow wetlands, a swamp where the waters of Beaver Creek never fail to flow. The creek slips out of the fake lake and dives into the dam, rushing downstream to downtown Bristol.

🚗 Bristol: Sugar Hollow Park

From I-81 Exit 13, go south on I-81 (US-58) for six miles to I-81 Exit 7. Turn right off the ramp and follow Old Airport Road for 0.1 miles. Turn right on US-11/19 (Lee Hwy.) and go north for a half mile to Sugar Hollow Park, on the left. Continue on the entrance road for 0.2 miles to Preston's Grove (not open for visitors) on the right and the Beaver Creek Dam on the left. Follow the park road for another half mile to the Sugar Hollow wetlands parking area, on the left. The 400-acre park includes trails, a campground, a picnic area, and playgrounds. Beyond the wetlands, a fee-entry area leads to creek-side picnic shelters and a half-mile trail reaching the four-foot-high Beaver Creek Cascades. From here, retrace the route to I-81 Exit 7.

Border Bash

Virginia's southern border may look straight, but it's not. Slight variations make it dip to the south near Danville then move slightly north before reaching Tennessee. Next, the border jogs up two miles and forms a crook in the line for another fifteen miles.

This big dent has become the "Offset" community of Tennessee's Sullivan and Johnson counties. And no one knows for sure how that crook got there.

But there's a legend that says a conniving woman gave surveyors some favors to alter the boundary. Another says surveyors were too drunk to draw a straight line. A third says iron-ore deposits interfered with compass readings. Possibly, too, there was confusion in having four or more lines drawn over several years to separate the territories of Virginia and Tennessee.

Thomas Jefferson's father, Peter Jefferson, halted a survey crew marking about 100 miles of the Virginia–North Carolina border in 1749. At a place Jefferson called "Steep Rock," the dividing line stopped on the border of present-day Tennessee.

Surveyor Dr. Thomas Walker tried to pick up where Jefferson left off. But Walker noted that Steep Rock in 1779 "could not be found, owing, we suppose to so much of the timber thereabout being since dead!"

Walker picked a new spot and headed west. So did Richard Henderson. But Henderson's line, surveyed for what was then North Carolina, did not match what Walker had completed for Virginia. Even so, both lines remained. And what lay between became a no-man's-land, especially at the Offset, where some settlers denied being citizens of any state to avoid taxes, the law, and military service.

West of the Offset, the City of Bristol was born in 1856 along the disputed border. It was actually two cities—a Bristol in Virginia, another in Tennessee—with the state line running down a shared Main Street.

In 1881, at a time when Virginia's Bristol was still called "Goodson," leaders from Bristol, Tennessee, passed a resolution officially marking the state boundary at the center of Main Street. But, not much later, hostility brewed on the border, largely over where companies could establish waterlines and exactly where the state line lay.

These disputes reached a boiling point during 1889 in what became known as Bristol's "Water Works War."

State Street in downtown Bristol

Much testimony was taken in the case, including a statement from an elderly woman who said she didn't want the state line moved because that would put her home in Virginia, and she had always heard that the climate was milder in Tennessee.

The Supreme Court ultimately ruled on a compromise, saying a survey in 1802–1803 had already properly marked the state line. Still, parts of that boundary were hard to find, so yet another survey had to be completed.

Bristol's Main Street became "State Street" in 1901 to match where the state line was officially placed, in the middle of the road. A few years later, a stunning show of unity arched above both Bristols: the landmark Bristol Sign, standing more than 50 feet tall and connecting the cities at State Street like a mammoth metallic handshake.

An armed militia from Tennessee faced another from Virginia. Each stood on opposite sides of a water ditch in the middle of Main Street. Virginia officials had just arrested Sam King of Tennessee for trying to install a waterline in Virginia. Now Goodson town officials wanted to lay another waterline, and Tennessee officials planned to arrest them for trespassing into Tennessee.

At the brink of a showdown, Officer James Cox of Goodson caught his foot on a water pipe and fell into the muddy ditch. Sullivan County Sheriff R. S. Cartwright also plopped into the mud. Then Cartwright laughed, seemingly at the absurdity of it all. And that laughter broke the day's tension.

The border bash was aborted. Still, the state line dispute remained, so Virginia and Tennessee took the matter to the Supreme Court to finally find out where they should be separated.

Bristol: State Street

From I-81 Exit 7, follow I-81 (US-58) south for six miles to I-81 Exit 1B. Then follow 2.5 miles into Bristol on Gate City Highway, which turns into West State Street, then State Street. The historic section of State Street lies east of the US-11E (Commonwealth Ave./Volunteer Pkwy.) intersection, reaching the Bristol Sign standing over the state line, at the railroad tracks. Erected in 1910 and moved to its present site in 1915, the sign is listed on historic landmark registers.

Hank's Last Ride

Nobody knows where Hank Williams died, not even Charles Carr, the chauffeur on Hank's last ride, as 1952 faded into 1953. Still, the mystery of Hank's final journey from Knoxville, Tennessee, to what should have been Canton, Ohio, has prompted people to pen songs, write books, and even board a bus for hundreds of miles.

The trip began at Knoxville's Andrew Johnson Hotel on December 31, 1952. The 17-year-old Carr got the job of driving the country singer's Cadillac through wintry weather as Hank lay in the backseat, doped up from a doctor's medication. Hank had a New Year's Day show in Canton, and if he missed it, he paid a fine. So Carr sped the car north along US-11W until he was stopped for a speeding ticket in Rutledge, Tennessee.

After that, Carr stopped for food . . . somewhere. And, somehow, Hank fans have come to think that he stopped at the Burger Bar in Bristol, Virginia. Carr asked Hank if he wanted something to eat or drink, and Hank said his final word—"No."

But, that event couldn't have happened at the Burger Bar. At the time of Hank's last ride, the Burger Bar building housed the Bristol Cleaners & Furriers.

The site was called "Snack King Restaurant" in 1957. It had become the Burger Bar by 1967. Hank's Cadillac would have, at least, passed by this building while going north on US-11/US-19. And, that seems fitting. Hank's honky-tonk music had descended from the style of Jimmie Rodgers, a singer who made his first record in 1927 in Bristol, Tennessee, just a couple blocks east of the Burger Bar.

For Bristol, the biggest Hank hoopla happened in 1998, when 30 people stopped on a tour bus followed by a five-car caravan, all thinking this was where Hank had said his final word. Flying a banner that proclaimed "Hank Williams' Final Journey," these Hank fans inspected the Burger Bar while on a jaunt to Oak Hill, West Virginia, the town where the singer was pronounced dead on New Year's Day, 1953.

Carr was not on that 1998 expedition. The Alabama businessman, then, had never retraced the path of Hank's last ride. But, in 1999, Carr questioned where Hank said "no" and where he picked up a relief driver, the late Donald Surface.

"It probably was Bluefield," Carr said. "For 40 years, I said it was Bristol, and that's where I thought it was."

The stop turned out to be the Dough Boy of Blue-field, West Virginia, about 100 miles north of the Burger Bar. A waitress, Hazel Wells Schultz, remembered that Hank's Cadillac stopped that night, and newspapers, just the day after Hank's death, had carried reports that Carr had stopped in Bluefield.

"We only gassed up one time," Carr said. "Wherever the restaurant was, I got a burger, and the cab-stand was there. And that's where we gassed up. Wherever that was is where I got Donald Surface."

But the ride didn't last long. Going just a few miles north of Bluefield, Carr noticed that "one of the covers" had slipped off Hank, that the singer had his hand on his heart, and that his hand was stiff. Hank's last ride had ended. He was dead at age 29.

Bristol: Burger Bar

The Burger Bar, 8 Piedmont Ave., stands immediately north of Bristol's State Street, about 0.2 miles west of the Bristol Sign. The city's *Birthplace of Country Music* mural, depicting Jimmie Rodgers, is painted on the side of the old Lark Amusements Building in the 800 block of State Street, one block west of the Burger Bar. Also pictured on the mural is the Carter Family, a group that also made its first recordings in Bristol in 1927. From here, retrace State Street/Gate City Hwy. for 2.3 miles to US-58 at I-81 Exit 1A.

Bristol's Burger Bar

Johnny and June

Johnny Cash showed up two days too early to note June Carter's birthday. He was also one month too late; June had died on May 15, 2003. The Man in Black, still, sat onstage at the Carter Fold, and he said he found peace in coming to his late wife's "old homeplace here on the banks of Clinch Mountain, where we spent so much time and had so much love for each other."

As early as 1962, Johnny and June walked together along the dirt roads at Poor Valley where June grew up. They played with June's young cousins, and they ate country suppers. "I was impressed," Johnny recalled. "I just fell in love with Poor Valley and Scott County."

Frequently, the singers returned to this close-knit community. They also played homecoming concerts at the Carter Fold, a venue built by June's cousins Joe and Janette Carter to honor the Carter Family, the musical trio of the siblings' parents, A. P. and Sara Carter, and June's mother, Maybelle Carter. Discovered in nearby Bristol, Tennessee, in 1927, the Carter Family became a million-selling success by the time June was born in the Maces Spring section of Poor Valley on June 23, 1929.

June was a tomboy, constantly climbing the trees of Clinch Mountain. While still a child, she joined the Carter Family, dancing and singing on such standards as "Keep on the Sunny Side" and "Will the Circle Be Unbroken?" June later sang with her sisters, Helen and Anita, and "Mother" Maybelle. She became friends with Hank Williams, and she was a godmother to Hank Williams, Jr. She also became a self-effacing ham, telling audiences lines like, "I've got my hair parted in the middle. Daddy says I used to do that to balance my brain."

The Virginia home of Johnny Cash and June Carter

Johnny Cash and his son John Carter at the Carter Fold

June Carter at the Carter Fold in 2000

By the 1960s, June sang with Johnny Cash, a rock 'n' roll pioneer and country music superstar. June steered Johnny off drugs. Then she married him in 1968. The couple lived in Hendersonville, Tennessee, but they also had the A-frame home of June's parents, Maybelle and Ezra "Eck" Carter, in Poor Valley. Johnny and June bought the house in 1981 on what Johnny called "the banks of Clinch Mountain."

The Cashes stayed in Virginia for up to three weeks at a time. Often, June scouted local flea markets and antique sales with her favorite cousin, Fern Carter Salyer. These cousins carted home so much loot that Johnny had to buy June a truck. Johnny, meanwhile, explored Clinch Mountain in a Jeep with June's cousin Joe Carter. But sometimes these men got into comical calamities, like once unknowingly running over a tree and noisily dragging it back down a mountain road.

Still, Johnny never met Joe's father, A. P. Carter, a songwriter and the leader of the Carter Family. A. P. died in 1960. Some years later, Johnny became the Carter Family's new musical patriarch. He reinspired

audiences with shows, records, and television appearances, and he often took Mother Maybelle and the Carter Sisters on the road with him. Johnny also escorted a frail Maybelle to the Carter Fold stage for her final concert with Sara Carter in 1977.

Johnny consistently broke a house rule. He played an electric guitar at the Carter Fold while other musicians had to abide by Janette Carter's acoustic-only policy. Johnny also played many shows by surprise, mentioned mainly by rumors. "I don't advertise that he's going to be here too much," Janette Carter once said. "It's foolish to advertise when you ain't got no place to sit people."

The Carter Fold ran out of chairs in 2000 when Johnny played a concert for more than 1,000 people. By then, his health had deteriorated from various ailments. He had been in a coma. But he still showed he could "Get Rhythm" and sing "Jackson" with June. That night, too, June said the couple was "hoping to retire" in Virginia. The crowd roared.

For the next two years, Johnny and June traveled

together to Poor Valley for June's birthday parties. They also promised to help restore the fallen-down cabin where June's father and uncles were born. But June died just as that old cabin was being dismantled.

Without June, Johnny looked weathered. Once towering among the pines of Clinch Mountain, he now sat in a wheelchair. His hands twitched. And he sounded choked up at the Carter Fold when he made that spiritual pilgrimage to mark June's birthday, two days too early, on June 21, 2003.

"The pain is so severe that there's no describing it," Johnny told his audience. "There's no way to tell exactly what the pain is. It's the big one. It's the biggest. When you lose your mate, the one you've been with all those years, I guarantee it's the big one. It hurts so bad. It hurts. It really hurts."

Johnny sang "Ring of Fire," a song June had written with Merle Kilgore. His crackling voice wavered. That singing, still, seemed to help his troubled soul. Staying in Virginia a few more days, he stopped again at the Carter Fold, singing a few more songs on July 5, his last concert anywhere.

Little more than three months later, just as that old Carter cabin was being restored, Johnny joined June at the family circle in the sky, Lord, in the sky.

Carter Cabin at Maces Spring

🚗 Maces Spring: Carter Fold & Maybelle Carter Homestead

From I-81 Exit 1A, head west on US-58, passing small waterfalls along the Ketron Branch of Cove Creek, on the left, after eight miles. Continue another ten miles and cross the North Fork of the Holston River. Then go another half mile and turn right on VA-709 at Hiltons (a village named for a local Hilton family). Go 0.1 miles, turn right on VA-614 (A. P. Carter Hwy.), and go three miles to the Carter Fold, A. P. Carter Museum, and A. P. Carter Birthplace Cabin, all on the left, at Maces Spring.

Continue for 0.7 miles to the privately owned former home of June Carter and Johnny Cash, also on the left; a marker in a roadside flower bed honors Mother Maybelle Carter. Go 0.8 miles beyond the house to the Mount Vernon United Methodist Church, where A. P. Carter, Sara Carter, Joe Carter, and Janette Carter are buried. A. P. Carter's gravestone, marked by a gold "Keep on the Sunny Side" record, stands about six rows from the back of the cemetery behind the church. Joe Carter's gravestone, nearby, is shaped like a guitar. From here, retrace the route to US-58 at Hiltons.

Muscles for Mussels

Muscles for Mussels

Clinch River rolls through Virginia with no reservoirs, from its headwaters near Tazewell to the Tennessee state line. The water flows free and healthy for more than 45 different kinds of mussels, creating one of the most diverse freshwater mussel habitats in the world.

Sometimes, there's a spill. In 1977, with no dam to hold back floodwaters, the river inundated the tiny town of Clinchport and wreaked havoc upstream at St. Paul. Later, St. Paul built a small dam and sealed off a troublesome channel but still kept the river flowing.

St. Paul pays tribute to the Clinch River with a cartoon mascot, the Mighty MusselMan. He rides a fish like a horse. This small-town superhero flexes his muscles for mussels, much like the real-life work of the Nature Conservancy, which has created a series of sanctuaries for rare mussels to thrive along the Clinch River.

Mussels are part of a river's natural filtering system. Enclosed between two protective shells, mussels feed on whatever's in the water. They consume pollutants. But about the only time a mussel makes a move is just after it's born.

Mother mussels release larvae—or baby mussels—with a puff in the water. To survive, these minuscule mussels must act like the Mighty MusselMan by taking a ride on a fish. They leech onto gills and travel for a couple of weeks, then drop to the streambed and grow up, essentially and always living near the same spot of silt or sand. Adult mussels can pull themselves on the river bottom with a long, muscular foot. But they move slower than snails, going only 100 feet during a lifetime of 75 years.

In the Clinch River, the strength of all mussels has been strained by the pollution of strip mines, industrial facilities, farming, and sewage treatment plants.

Sometimes, there's a spill. In 1967, nearly a dozen miles of mussels and more than 200,000 fish were killed on the Clinch River by a leak of coal-ash slurry by the Appalachian Power Company in Carbo, upstream from St. Paul.

But, near Clinchport, there was a spill of a good kind. The Virginia Department of Game and Inland Fisheries planted hundreds of speck-sized wavyrayed lampmussels in the river in 2001. It marked the first time in Virginia that cultured mussels were released into an existing wild population.

Clinch River near Clinchport

🚗 Clinchport: Clinch River

From VA-709 at Hiltons, turn right on US-58 and continue west for 5.3 miles to US-58's junction with US-23 near Big Moccasin Gap, a natural passage through Clinch Mountain marked by a wayside park. Big Moccasin Gap was named in the 1700s by pioneers who found the prints of moccasins worn by Indians. From the gap at Weber City (a town named for a skit on the "Amos 'n Andy" radio show), continue west on US-58, passing Gate City (a town named for being a gateway in the mountains). Cross the Clinch River bridge at 11.5 miles. Continue another 1.5 miles west and turn right on VA-65. Go one mile to the Clinchport canoe and fishing access, on the right.

Tale of the Tornado

It might have sounded like a train, but it couldn't have been. There was no railroad in Rye Cove. The nearest track passed near Clinchport, about eight miles south along the Clinch River.

This great noise was a howling wind. With it, the sky grew dark like night. "Then it got real light," remembered Lucille Cowden Necessary. "And the lumber started hitting us."

This was a tornado, the worst tornado tragedy in Virginia history. On May 2, 1929, the whirlwind ransacked Rye Cove in the shape of a dirty black cloud, whipping down rocky fields and arriving at the valley's Rye Cove Consolidated School just after recess.

Inside the school, ten-year-old Lucille watched a window fly toward her desk. She ducked. Then she blacked out as the two-story wooden schoolhouse was lifted into the cyclone. The schoolhouse spun and shattered, spitting students, teachers, books, and desks back down to the ground.

Lucille awoke in the twister's trap of splintered glass and boards, all that was left of the school. She was pierced by nails. She had a broken foot and a severed finger—and she was one of the lucky ones. Other kids screamed as flames shot out of the wreckage from an overturned stove. Some were burned by acid in the school's science lab.

Rye Cove in May

Red Cross Cabin, now part of a park in Rye Cove

That night, Lucille went to sleep trying to block out the clamor of hammers. Coffins were being made for those who were killed, a total of 12 students and one teacher.

The American Red Cross constructed a log cabin for a relief center. Musician A. P. Carter of the Carter Family also helped recovery efforts and penned a song, "The Cyclone of Rye Cove," which spun a tale of the tornado. But the following year would be a lost time, with no school for the 155 students of Rye Cove.

Haunted by memories of their real-life nightmare, children in the valley developed a habit of holding down their heads, afraid to look at the sky.

Maybe this is the end of the world, Lucille thought. Just days before, she had been sitting in church in Rye Cove when the preacher gave a sermon saying that End Times were near and that some would be taken up and some left behind.

The tornado hit around 1:00 P.M., but two hours passed before outside help arrived in isolated Rye Cove. Next, it was a challenge to evacuate the wounded in wagons on Rye Cove's muddy, rutted road to Clinchport, where trains could rush to hospitals in Bristol, Virginia, and Kingsport, Tennessee.

🚗 Scott County: Rye Cove

From the Clinch River access at Clinchport, follow VA-65 (Clinch River Hwy.) northeast for 3.5 miles. Turn left on VA-649 (Rye Cove Memorial Rd.) and follow for 2.7 miles to the site of Rye Cove School, on the right. The former school's belfry, perched on bricks in the schoolyard, serves as a memorial, listing names of tornado victims. The old Red Cross cabin, renovated in 2004, stands beside the school at a small park. From here, retrace VA-649 to VA-65 and follow 4.5 miles southwest to US-58.

Natural Tunnel

Nothing's haunting the Natural Tunnel except its old name, Natural Bridge. That's what the rocky landmark was dubbed for a good part of the 19th century.

It is not—to repeat, not—the same place as the Natural Bridge of Rockbridge County, Virginia. Only, not everybody knows that. People often call wanting to check into the hotel or look for the wax museum, only to find that neither exists at Natural Tunnel State Park.

Once, too, the daughter of a 102-year-old woman from Georgia called the park office, saying her mother wanted to see the rock formation just one more time before she died. Park officials made every effort to oblige, even to the point of operating the chairlift to the tunnel during the off-season. But then the family cancelled just two days before the planned visit and said they had made a mistake. They were actually thinking about revisiting Natural Bridge.

Longtime Natural Tunnel State Park Manager Craig Seaver blamed such mix-ups on "more of a marketing problem than anything else."

But factor in history. Decades before the first train passed through the Natural Tunnel in 1890, Matthew

Natural Tunnel

Carey called the formation "Natural Bridge" on an 1814 map. For the next few decades, the dark passage through Purchase Ridge retained at least some reference as a "Natural Bridge," once a generic term for any arch-type rock formation.

The Natural Bridge gives its name to Rockbridge County. And it stands like a doorway, with one side leading to the Shenandoah Valley and the other opening to Virginia's Southern Blue Ridge Highlands. Thomas Jefferson owned the Natural Bridge and called it "the most sublime of nature's works."

The Natural Tunnel sits in the woods of Scott County. It has not been owned by anybody particularly famous, but it does form a general gateway between Virginia's coal-mining region and the slant-sided farms of the Clinch Valley.

In many early descriptions, Natural Tunnel was mentioned with seemingly obligatory comparisons to Natural Bridge. Lewis Preston Summers's 1903 *History of Southwest Virginia* contains a passage by writer Charles B. Coale, who notes that the landmark is "not so perfect as that of Rockbridge county, but is much grander in proportion and is laid out upon much more stupendous scale."

Make that quite stupendous, even if the 850-foot-long Natural Tunnel can't claim half the fame as the 90-foot-long Natural Bridge. It is, indeed, grander in proportion. The curved limestone walls outside Natural Tunnel stand about 400 feet, compared to Natural Bridge's rise of 215 feet.

🚗 Scott County: Natural Tunnel State Park

From VA-65 at Clinchport, continue west on US-58 for 1.2 miles. Turn right on VA-871 and follow for one mile to Natural Tunnel State Park, on the right. The 850-acre park features a playground, picnic areas, a visitor center, a swimming pool, and a campground. A chairlift and trails lead to Natural Tunnel. Other attractions include the replica of a blockhouse, made to resemble the kind of 18th-century forts that once stood along the Wilderness Road in Southwest Virginia.

Cold War

Cold War

For months, the Civil War interrupted the peace of Powell Valley. Once, Federal troops stomped through the quiet town of Jonesville and torched the Lee County Courthouse. Another time, in a unique case of friendly fire, the Confederates of the 64th Virginia Infantry left some embers unattended and accidentally burned some cabins while occupying the Jonesville Methodist Campground.

Fortunately, no flames touched the campground's wooden shed. That landmark has been used for annual prayer meetings since the 1820s. Still, that shed was without a prayer in 1863 and 1864 as the war lingered. Church leaders opted to meet elsewhere, fearing a surprise attack by the Union Army.

Such action arrived in bitter cold at the end of 1863. Union Maj. Charles H. Beeres tried to occupy tiny Jonesville with about 400 men in the 16th Illinois Cavalry. Beeres's forces made a stand at the Dickinson-Milbourn House, a Federal-style brick home built on a knoll in the 1840s for prosperous landowner Benjamin Dickinson.

The news of Beeres's arrival made it to Lt. Col. Auburn L. Pridemore, the Confederate commander

The Dickinson-Milbourn House at Jonesville

of the 64th Virginia Cavalry. Pridemore moved a force of 230 men into Jonesville from the east. Brig. Gen. William E. "Grumble" Jones marched north to Jonesville with more Confederate troops from Tennessee. The ensuing clash between North and South became the Battle of Jonesville on January 3, 1864.

Talk about a cold war; it was snowing, and temperatures dipped below zero. At least one of Jones's men froze to death even before making it to Jonesville. Other Confederates suffered frostbite after splashing through the cold Clinch River and climbing icy mountain roads.

Guns and cannons, by contrast, blazed hot. Clearly, the Union forces were trapped. Pridemore had blocked routes to the east and north. Jones had cut off roads to the south and west. And Beeres surrendered, giving up three pieces of light artillery, hundreds of men, and more than 20 six-mule teams.

The frigid fight left dead and wounded on both sides. But, for a while, there would be peace in Powell Valley again.

🚗 Jonesville: Dickinson-Milbourn House & Jonesville Methodist Campground

From the junction of US-58 and VA-871 near Natural Tunnel, follow US-58 west for 3.5 miles to Duffield (named for a local Duff family). Turn left on US-58 and continue west, reaching an overlook at the crest of Powell Mountain in 4.5 miles. Down the mountain, in two miles, reach Stickleyville (named for early settler Vastine Stoekli).

At 13 miles west of Stickleyville (or 23 miles west of the Natural Tunnel exit), reach the Lee County Courthouse on US-58 at Jonesville and turn left. A cemetery with the graves of Civil War soldiers stands 0.2 miles west of the courthouse. At 0.4 miles west of the cemetery, the privately owned Dickinson-Milbourn House stands on the right, across from Jonesville Middle School. Continue on US-58 for one mile west of the school. The Jonesville Methodist Campground stands near the VA-652 intersection at a historic marker, on the right. Both the house and the campground are listed on historic landmark registers.

Pioneer Graves

Joseph Martin charged into Virginia's unknown wilderness, gambling that he could safely settle the isolated Powell Valley. The young man started with a challenge from Dr. Thomas Walker to claim 21,000 acres of land. In 1750, Walker had surveyed Powell Valley with Ambrose Powell, a hunter who carved his name on a tree and later inspired subsequent travelers to name Powell Mountain, Powell River, and the Powell Valley for him in what is now Lee County, Virginia.

Martin won his own name on a creek. Leaving Albemarle County near Charlottesville, Virginia, he raced hundreds of miles in 1769 and got lost in the woods. But he still beat a competing expedition by more than two weeks. That March, he set up a fort. He planted corn. He explored. But just as the corn crop ripened, Indians attacked. Martin fled and didn't return to Powell Valley for six years. He then built another fort along the same creek, and he attracted fellow pioneers, who shopped and slept at "Martin's Station." But along came another raid, and Martin was gone again after June 1776.

Such were the perils of Powell Valley. For pioneers like Martin, it was tempting to try to tame this terri-

Monument at Caylor in Lee County

Ely Mound rises just ahead of the barn near Rose Hill.

tory. But conflicts with Native Americans seemed to always make the area impossible to settle.

Famed frontiersman Daniel Boone personally discovered the dangers. Boone came through the Powell Valley in 1773—a time when Martin wasn't around—while wandering west with family and friends.

On the morning of October 10, somewhere in the woods, Indians ambushed Boone's 16-year-old son James Boone and 17-year-old Henry Russell at the boys' small campsite. Both boys were shot through the hips and stabbed with knives. Both had their fingernails and toenails ripped out. Finally and fatally, both boys were tomahawked. The Indians killed three more campers, another was kidnapped, and two managed to escape.

A petty thief found the boys' bloody remains after he ran off from Daniel Boone's main camp nearby. The thief ran back and alerted Boone's group. They immediately prepared for an attack, stacking trees and making a quick fort. But the Indians did not return. Boone's family buried James and Henry together in an unmarked grave and then retreated east to the Clinch Valley.

Historians agree that the murders of 1773 slowed Daniel Boone's push to the west. But historians disagree over where the murders happened, on either the east or west side of the county, and where the boys were subsequently buried. Some say it was along Wallen's Creek near Stickleyville, the site of a state historical marker. Others contend it was in the west at

Martin's Station replica at Wilderness Road State Park

Caylor, where, in 1951, a privately funded stone monument was erected with a description of the murders, titled "Pioneer Graves."

What is known, without an argument, is that Indians are buried in graves all over Lee County. Many lie in raised mounds, popping out of Powell Valley like perfectly rounded hills. One such grave site, called the Ely Mound, remained unexplored until 1877, when a leg-endary excavation for the Peabody Museum of American Archeology and Ethnology helped theorize that Indians had built the mound between 1200 and 1650.

Local resident Charles B. Johnson discovered the skeletons of two Indian children below the top of the 19-foot-high Ely Mound. Then Professor Lucius H. Cheney climbed into a six-foot-long shaft and made an announcement that excited a crowd of onlookers.

He said there was an entire skeleton that could be saved, but it would have to come out delicately, piece by piece.

Several spectators slipped to the side of the excavation to get a better look. But they rushed so fast and with such force that a section of the grassy mound collapsed. The excavators, Cheney and Johnson, were suddenly trapped inside the tomb!

It took about 20 minutes to pull out Cheney. The earth had fallen on his neck and the back of his head, killing him. Johnson was bruised but alive, and he finished excavating the Ely Mound a week later with Carr.

The Ely Mound owes its name to the family of Robert Ely, a prominent farmer who built a 12-room mansion called "Elydale" in the 1870s. In the 1990s, Ely's mansion became part of the Wilderness Road State Park, the site of a life-size replica of Martin's Station. The park's fort represents what Joseph Martin constructed in 1775 when he returned to Powell Valley: a stockade with a half dozen cabins.

For the record, Martin didn't give up on Powell Valley after 1776. The pioneer established a new Martin's Station in 1783, this time a few miles west of the original site. Five prosperous years later, he sold off his land claims and retired at the foot of Virginia's mountains. His grave lies there at Martinsville, a city named for him, just as his name remains in Powell Valley at Martin Creek.

Rose Hill/Ewing: Wilderness Road State Park & Ely Mound

From Jonesville Methodist Campground at VA-652, follow US-58 west for 12.7 miles. Turn left at US-58 Business at Rose Hill and go 0.2 miles to a historic marker, on the right, noting the original site of Martin's Station, near Martin Creek. Continue west for three miles through Rose Hill to another historic marker, noting the site of the Ely Mound, located across US-58 (to the north), near a barn.

Continue west for 2.1 miles to Ewing (a place named for early settler Samuel Ewing). Turn right on VA-724 and go 0.1 miles. Turn left on US-58 and head west for 4.3 miles to Caylor (a name that should actually be "Taylor," for local landowners). Turn left on VA-684 and go 0.1 miles to the Pioneer Graves monument, on the right. Return to US-58 and go one mile to reach Wilderness Road State Park, on the right, at VA-690. The 200-acre park includes trails, a visitor center, and a picnic area.

Beyond the state park, continue west on US-58 for 6.7 miles. Go across Station Creek (site of the third Martin's Station) near the campground entrance of Cumberland Gap National Historical Park to reach the western terminus of the Wilderness Road Trail, a recreation path that parallels US-58. Covered with crushed gravel, the Wilderness Road Trail links the state park with the national park by following the former corridor of the Louisville & Nashville Railroad.

Bluegrass

Daniel Boone dreamed of the bluegrass of Kentucky—the untilled green, the wild turkey, the deer, the bear, the elk. It all waited to the west, beyond the ocean of the Appalachian Mountains.

But getting there seemed such a struggle. In 1767, the frontiersman stomped through the rocky Breaks Canyon on the Big Sandy River. But that area was too rough. Two years later, Boone made a trip to Kentucky through Cumberland Gap, a natural notch on a path used by animals and Indians. Hunter Gabriel Arthur became the first white man to walk through the Cumberland Gap in 1674 after being captured by Shawnees. But this cut in Cumberland Mountain remained a dormant doorway until 1750.

That year, Dr. Thomas Walker led a crew through the gap on a real estate expedition. The governor's council in Williamsburg granted Walker's group, the Loyal Company, a title to 800,000 acres west of the Appalachians in what became known as Kentucky. Walker returned with a journal bragging about coal deposits, buffalo, and bountiful fields.

The gap was named for William Augustus, the Duke of Cumberland and the son of King George II of England. But there would be no rush through this "Gateway to the West," at least not just yet. In the 1760s, Kentucky became closed to further settlement and exploration due to the French and Indian War.

Then came Boone. The Pennyslvania native's first trip to Kentucky's bluegrass fields teased his imagination. He saw great herds of buffalo, and he returned often, even longing to settle in that mysterious, virgin land.

Boone's knowledge of the Bluegrass and the narrow route getting there earned him a job in 1775. That year, the Transylvania Company made a deal with the Cherokee to buy millions of acres in Kentucky. Immediately, Boone and a group of 30 men marked the Wilderness Road, or "Boone's Trace," through dark forests to Kentucky.

This area soon evolved into Virginia's vast "County of Kentucky," stretching west to the Mississippi River. Thousands pulled wagons along Boone's Trace, especially after 1784, when writer John Filson described Kentucky as "the most extraordinary country that the sun enlightens with his celestial beams."

The Bluegrass grew. In 1792, what was briefly the "County of Kentucky" became a "Commonwealth,"

Fort McCook overlooking the Cumberland Gap

Alexander Arthur, who named it for the Middlesborough of England. Arthur acquired capital from English investors, and in 1889 he began to develop coal-mining, iron ore, and timber interests. Middlesborough grew from 50 people to 10,000 in less than eight months. And it all looked swell until a London bank went belly-up in 1890. Then came a fire. Then the Panic of 1893 took finances on a continuing crash.

Middlesboro had already experienced another crash millions of years earlier. A meteor dropped out of the sky and formed the three-mile-wide valley where the city grew. Possibly, that crash was similar to how a space rock slammed the Chesapeake Bay, slightly north of Cape Henry. At least, drawing a line between the two craters shows that meteors may have marked where Virginia should begin and end.

In the west, Virginia ends on a mountain. Roughly 500 miles away from the Atlantic Coast, even beyond the Cumberland Gap, the western tip of the Old Dominion overlooks the Bluegrass State. A wooden pavilion marks this spot, quietly hidden in the woods of the Cumberland Gap National Historical Park, a natural bookend on the trail from beach to bluegrass.

🚗 Cumberland Gap: Cumberland Gap National Historical Park

From the campground entrance at Cumberland Gap National Historical Park, continue west on US-58 to enter Tennessee in 1.2 miles. In another

just like Virginia. By then, Kentucky had been divided into three smaller counties, and the population of what became the Bluegrass State had reached more than 100,000, enough to qualify for statehood.

But Kentucky turned unkind for Boone. More than once, Shawnees captured the hunter. And, for years, he fought in court to keep his land claims. By 1800, a disgusted Boone left Kentucky for good.

Cumberland Gap remained a gateway. It was called the "Gibraltar of America" during the Civil War and was considered a strategic passage to both the Confederacy and the Union. Soldiers built earthworks and stripped trees off Cumberland Mountain to make way for cannonballs. Still, little happened. The biggest battles, likely, were waged against boredom and starvation.

Then came Middlesboro. Settled along the gap's western border, this Kentucky city was first spelled "Middlesborough." That extra "ugh" came from

Tri-State Marker, where Virginia ends

Walkway to Pinnacle Overlook at the "Garden of Gazes"

300 yards, turn right on North Cumberland Drive (the Cumberland Gap, Tennessee, exit) and go 300 yards, passing back into Virginia, to the Daniel Boone Parking Area, on the right.

From the kiosk, the uphill trail through Cumberland Gap runs about one mile to the saddle of the gap. There, on the left, use the Tri-State Trail and go 0.6 miles to the wooden pavilion at the Tri-State Peak, where the boundary of Kentucky, Tennessee, and Virginia is marked by concrete, stones, and brass plates.

To reach the national park visitor center from the Daniel Boone Parking Area, return to US-58 and go 0.2 miles, veering right on US-25E, and pass through the Cumberland Gap Tunnel. Exit immediately to the visitor center at Middlesboro. From here, Pinnacle Road leads to the Pinnacle Overlook, a site actually located in Virginia but reached by car by going through Kentucky. During the 1930s, the Skyland Company promoted the view at the Pinnacle as the "Garden of Gazes."

Resources

Abingdon Convention & Visitor Bureau
335 Cummings St.
Abingdon, VA 24210
(800) 435-3440 / (276) 676-2282
www.abingdon.com

Attucks Theatre
1010 Church St.
Norfolk, VA 23510
(757) 622-4763
www.attuckstheatre.org

Barter Theatre
133 W. Main St.
Abingdon, VA 24210
(276) 628-3991
www.bartertheatre.com

Berry Hill
3105 River Rd.
South Boston, VA 24592
(434) 517-7000
www.berryhillinn.com

Birthplace of Country Music Alliance
www.birthplaceofcountrymusic.org

Blue Ridge Music Center
Blue Ridge Parkway, Mile 213
(276) 236-5309
www.blueridgemusiccenter.org

Blue Ridge Passage Resort
4037 Jeb Stuart Hwy.
Meadows of Dan, VA 24120
(866) 347-3767 / (276) 952-3456
www.blueridgepassageresort.com

Brunswick County Museum
228 N. Main St.
Lawrenceville, VA 23868
(866) 783-9768 / (434) 848-0964
www.tourbrunswick.org

Burger Bar
8 Piedmont Ave.
Bristol, VA 24201
(276) 466-6200

Carroll County Historical Museum
515 N. Main St.
Hillsville, VA 24343
(276) 728-4113

Carter Family Fold
P.O. Box 111
Hiltons, VA 24258
(276) 386-6054
www.carterfamilyfold.org

Cavalier Hotel
Oceanfront and 42nd Street
Virginia Beach, VA 23451
(800) 446-8199 / (757) 425-8555
www.cavalierhotel.com

Chateau Morrisette Winery
P.O. Box 766
Meadows of Dan, VA 24120
(540) 593-2865
www.chateaumorrisette.com

Childrens Museum of Virginia
221 High St.
Portsmouth, VA 23704
(757) 393-5258
www.childrensmuseumva.com

Chrysler Museum of Art
245 W. Olney Rd.
Norfolk, VA 23510
(757) 664-6200
www.chrysler.org

Clarksville/Lake Country Chamber of Commerce
105 Second St.
Clarksville, VA 23927
(800) 557-5582 / (434) 374-2436
www.clarksvilleva.org

Commodore Theatre
421 High St.
Portsmouth, VA 23704
(757) 393-6962
www.commodoretheatre.com

Courthouse Galleries Museum
420 High St.
Portsmouth, VA 23704
(757) 393-8543
www.courthousegalleries.com

Cumberland Gap National Historical Park
P.O. Box 1848
Middlesboro, KY 40965
(606) 248-2817
www.nps.gov/cuga

Daniel Boone Wilderness Trail Association
P.O. Box 757
Gate City, VA 24251
www.danielboonetrail.com

Danville Museum of Fine Arts & History
975 Main St.
Danville, VA 24541
(434) 793-5644
www.danvillemuseum.org

Danville Science Center
677 Craghead St.
Danville, VA 24541
(434) 791-5160
www.dsc.smv.org

Danville Welcome Center
645 River Park Dr.
Danville, VA 24540
(434) 793-4636
www.visitdanville.com

Fairy Stone State Park
967 Fairy Stone Lake Dr.
Stuart, VA 24171
(276) 930-2424
www.dcr.virginia.gov/state_parks/fai.shtml

First Landing State Park
2500 Shore Dr.
Virginia Beach, VA 23451
(757) 412-2300
www.dcr.virginia.gov/state_parks/fir.shtml

Francis Land House Historic Site & Gardens
3131 Virginia Beach Blvd.
Virginia Beach, VA 23452
(757) 431-4000

Galax Tourism
111 E. Grayson St.
Galax, VA 24333
(276) 238-8130
www.ingalax.net

Grayson County Tourism & 1908 Courthouse
107 E. Main St.
Independence, VA 24348
(276) 773-3711
www.graysoncountyva.com

Grayson Highlands State Park
829 Grayson Highland Lane
Mouth of Wilson, VA 24363
(276) 579-7092
www.dcr.virginia.gov/state_parks/gra.shtml

Great Dismal Swamp National Wildlife Refuge
3100 Desert Rd.
Suffolk, VA 23434
(757) 986-3705
www.fws.gov/northeast/greatdismalswamp

Green Cove Depot
41259 Green Cove Rd.
Damascus, VA 24236
(276) 388-3386

Harmon Museum
5122 Carrollton Pike
Woodlawn, VA 24381
(276) 236-4884
www.harmonstore.com

Historic Boydton's Renaissance, Inc.
461 Madison St.
Boydton, VA 23917
(434) 738-0113
www.boydton.org

J.E.B. Stuart Birthplace, Inc.
P.O. Box 240
Ararat, VA 24053
(276) 251-1833
www.jebstuart.org

Jeff Matthews Memorial Museum
606 W. Stuart Drive
Galax, VA 24333
(276) 236-7874
www.jeffmatthewsmuseum.org

John H. Kerr Dam and Reservoir
1930 Mays Chapel Rd.
Boydton, VA 23917
(434) 738-6143
www.saw.usace.army.mil/jhkerr/index.htm

MacArthur Memorial
MacArthur Square
Norfolk, VA 23510
(757) 441-2965
www.macarthurmemorial.org

Mabry Mill
266 Mabry Mill Rd. Southeast
Meadows of Dan, VA 24120
(276) 952-2947

Martha Washington Inn
150 W. Main St.
Abingdon, VA 24210
(276) 628-3161
www.marthawashingtoninn.com

Martinsville-Henry County Office of Tourism
P.O. Box 631
Martinsville, VA 24114
(276) 403-5940
www.visitmartinsville.com

Martinsville Speedway
340 Speedway Rd.
Ridgeway, VA 24148
(877) 722-3849
www.martinsvillespeedway.com

Mayberry Trading Post
883 Mayberry Church Rd.
Meadows of Dan, VA 24120
(276) 952-2155

Moonlite Theatre
17555 Lee Hwy.
Abingdon, VA 24210
(276) 628-7881
www.moonlitetheatre.com

Mountain Music Museum
Bristol Mall
Bristol, VA 24201
(276) 645-0035
www.mountainmusicmuseum.org

Mount Rogers National Recreation Area
P.O. Box 303
Marion, VA 24354
(800) 628-7202 / (276) 783-5196
www.fs.fed.us/r8/gwj/mr/

Mount Trashmore Park
310 Edwin Dr.
Virginia Beach, VA 23462
(757) 473-5237

Natural Tunnel State Park
Rt. 3, Box 250
Duffield, VA 24244-9361
(276) 940-2674
http://www.dcr.virginia.gov/state_parks/nat.shtml

Nauticus: The National Maritime Center
One Waterside Drive
Norfolk, VA 23510
(800) 664-1080 / (757) 664-1000
www.nauticus.org

New River Trail State Park
176 Orphanage Dr.
Foster Falls, VA 24360
(276) 699-6778
www.dcr.virginia.gov/state_parks/new.shtml

Norfolk Botanical Garden
6700 Azalea Garden Rd.
Norfolk, VA 23518
(757) 441-5830
www.norfolkbotanicalgarden.org

Norfolk Convention and Visitors Bureau
232 E. Main St.
Norfolk, VA 23510
(800) 368-3097 / (757) 664-6620
www.norfolkcvb.com

Occoneechee State Park
1192 Occoneechee Park Rd.
Clarksville, VA 23927
(434) 374-2210
www.dcr.virginia.gov/state_parks/occ.shtml

Old Cape Henry Lighthouse
583 Atlantic Ave.
Fort Story, VA 23459
(757) 422-9421
www.apva.org/capehenry

Old Coast Guard Station
24th St. and Atlantic Ave.
Virginia Beach, VA 23458
(757) 422-1587
www.oldcoastguardstation.com

Patrick County Historical Museum
116 W. Blue Ridge St.
Stuart, VA 24171
(276) 694-2840
www.patcovahistory.org

Patrick Henry National Monument
1250 Red Hill Rd.
Brookneal, VA 24528
(800) 514-7463
www.redhill.org

Planters Peanut Center
308 W. Washington St.
Suffolk, VA 23434
(757) 539-4411
www.suffolkpeanuts.com

Portsmouth Naval Shipyard Museum
High Street Landing
Portsmouth, VA 23704
(757) 393-8591
www.portsnavalmuseums.com

Portsmouth Visitor Center
6 Crawford Pkwy.
Portsmouth, VA 23704
(800) 767-8782 / (757) 393-5111
www.portsva.com

Prestwould Foundation
P.O. Box 872
Clarksville, VA 23927
(434) 374-8672

Rawls Museum Arts
22376 Linden St.
Courtland, VA 23837
(757) 653-0754
www.rawlsarts.com

Rex Theater
113 Grayson St.
Galax, VA 24333
www.rextheatergalax.com

Reynolds Homestead
463 Homestead Lane
Critz, VA 24082
(276) 694-7181
www.reynoldshomestead.vt.edu

Riddick's Folly House Museum
510 N. Main St.
Suffolk, VA 23434
(757) 934-1390
www.riddicksfolly.org

South Boston-Halifax County Museum
1540 Wilborn Ave.
South Boston, VA 24592
(434) 572-9200
www.sbhcmuseum.org

South Boston Speedway
1188 James D. Hagood Hwy.
South Boston, VA 24592
(877) 440-1540 / (434) 572-4947
www.southbostonspeedway.com

South Hill Tourist Information Center
201 S. Mecklenburg Ave.
South Hill, VA 23970
(800) 524-4347 / (434) 447-4547
www.southhillchamber.com

Southampton Agriculture and Forestry Museum
26315 Heritage Lane
Courtland, VA 23837
(757) 653-9554

Staunton River State Park
1170 Staunton Trail
Scottsburg, VA 24589-9636
(434) 572-4623
www.dcr.virginia.gov/state_parks/sta.shtml

St. Paul's Episcopal Church
201 St. Paul's Blvd.
Norfolk, VA 23510
(757) 627-4353

Suffolk Museum
118 Bosley Ave.
Suffolk, VA 23434
(757) 923-2371

Suffolk Seaboard Station Railroad Museum
326 N. Main St.
Suffolk, VA 23434
(757) 923-4750

Suffolk Visitor Center
321 N. Main St.
Suffolk, VA 23434
(866) 733-7835 / (757) 923-3880
www.suffolk-fun.com

Tobacco Farm Life Museum
306 W. Main St.
South Hill, VA 23970
(434) 447-2551

Village View
221 Briggs St.
(434) 634-2475
Emporia, VA 23847

Virginia Aquarium & Marine Science Center
717 General Booth Blvd.
Virginia Beach, VA 23451
(757) 385-3474

Virginia Beach Visitor Information Center
2100 Parks Ave.
Virginia Beach, VA 23451
(800) 822-3224 / (757) 437-4919
www.vbfun.com

Virginia's Heritage Music Trail
www.thecrookedroad.org

Virginia Museum of Natural History
21 Starling Ave.
Martinsville, VA 24112
(276) 634-4141
www.vmnh.net

Virginia Sports Hall of Fame
206 High St.
Portsmouth, VA 23704
(757) 393-8031
www.virginiasportshalloffame.com

Wilderness Road State Park
Rt. 2, Box 115
Ewing, VA 24248
(276) 445-3065
www.dcr.virginia.gov/state_parks/wil.shtml

William King Regional Arts Center
415 Academy Drive
Abingdon, VA 24212
(276) 628-5005
www.wkrac.org

Bibliography

Books

Anderson-Green, Paula Hathaway. *A Hot-Bed of Musicians: Traditional Music in the Upper New River Valley-Whitetop Region.* Knoxville: The University of Tennessee Press, 2002.

Beaudry, Mary C. *Colonizing the Virginia Frontier: Fort Christanna and Governor Spotswood's Indian Policy.* Boston: Boston University Archeological Studies Program, August 1981.

Bracey, Susan. *Life by the Roaring Roanoke: A History of Mecklenburg County, Virginia."* Mecklenburg County, Va.: The Mecklenburg County Bicentennial Commission, 1977.

Brent, Maria Campbell. *Taming Yellow Creek: Alexander Arthur, The Yellow Creek Canal & Middlesborough, Kentucky.* Lexington, Ky.: Kentucky Archaeological Survey, Education Series No. 5, 2002.

Brown, Douglas Summers, ed. *Sketches of Greensville County Virginia 1650-1967.* Emporia, Va.: The Riparian Woman's Club, 1968.

Brubaker III, John H. *The Last Capitol: Danville, Virginia and the Final Days of the Confederacy.* Danville, Va.: Danville Museum of Fine Arts and History, 1979.

Bucklen, Mary Kegley, and Larrie L. Bucklen. *County Courthouses of Virginia Old and New.* Charleston, W.Va.: Pictorial Histories Publishing Company, 1988.

Butt, Marshall W. *Portsmouth Under Four Flags: 1752-1970.* Portsmouth, Va.: by the author, 1971.

Cohen, Stan. *Historic Springs of the Virginias: A Pictorial History.* Charleston, W.Va.: Pictorial Histories Publishing Co., 1981.

Curtis, Claude D. *Three Quarters of a Century at Martha Washington College.* Bristol, Tenn.: King Printing Co., 1928.

Dabney, Virginius. *Virginia: The New Dominion.* Garden City, N.Y.: Doubleday & Co., Inc., 1971.

Dawidziak, Mark. *The Barter Theatre Story: Love Made Visible.* Boone, N.C.: Appalachian Consortium Press, 1982.

Donleavy, Kevin. *Strings of Life—Conversations with Old-Time Musicians from Virginia and North Carolina.* Blacksburg, Va.: Pocahontas Press, Inc., 2004.

Draper, Lyman C., LL.D, and Ted Franklin Belue, ed. *The Life of Daniel Boone.* Mechanicsburg, Penn.: Stackpole Books, 1998.

Drewry, William Sidney. *The Southampton Insurrection.* Murfreesboro, N.C.: Johnson Publishing Co., 1968.

Dunn Jr., Joseph W., and Barbara S. Lyle. *Virginia Beach: Wish You Were Here.* Norfolk, Va.: The Donning Company/Publishers, 1983.

Edmunds, Pocahontas Wight. *Tales of the Virginia Coast.* n.p.: by the author, 1950.

Elizabeth River Project. *Elizabeth River Restoration and Conservation: A Watershed Action Plan.* Revised second edition. Portsmouth, Va.: Elizabeth River Project, 2002.

Eubank, Robert C. *Bits and Pieces: First Ruritan Club.* Zuni, Va.: Pearl Line Press, 2002.

Fields, Bettye-Lou, ed. *Grayson County: A History in Words and Pictures.* Independence, Va.: Grayson County Historical Society, 1976.

Fleenor, Lawrence J. *Driving the Wilderness Trail.* Gate City, Va.: Daniel Boone Wilderness Trail Association, Inc., 2000.

Foster, Stephen William. *The Past Is Another Country: Representation, Historical Consciousness, and Resistance in the Blue Ridge.* Los Angeles: University of California Press, 1988.

Ginther, Herman. *Captain Staunton's River.* Richmond, Va.: The Dietz Press, Inc., 1968.

Goodwin, Doris Kearns. *No Ordinary Time: Franklin and Eleanor Roosevelt: The Home Front in World War II.* New York: Touchstone, 1994.

Gregory, G. Howard. *History of the Wreck of the Old 97.* Danville, Va.: by the author, 1992.

Hagemann, James A. *The Heritage of Virginia.* Norfolk, Va.: The Donning Co. Publishers, 1986.

Hall, Louise Fortune. *A History of Damascus 1793-1950.* Abingdon, Va.: John Anderson Press, 1950.

Hall, Ronald W. *The Carroll County Courthouse Tragedy.* Hillsville, Va.: Carroll County Historical Society, 1997.

Hanson, Raus McDill. *Virginia Place Names.* Verona, Va.: McClure Press, 1969.

Hobbs, Kermit, and William A. Paquette. *Suffolk: A Pictorial History.* Norfolk, Va.: The Donning Company/Publishers, 1987.

Holloday, Mildred M. *History of Portsmouth.* File at Wilson History Room, Portsmouth Public Library, Portsmouth, Va.

Holston Territory Genealogical Society. *Families of Washington County and Bristol Virginia 1776-1996.* Waynesville, N.C.: Don Mills, Inc., 1996.

Hume, Ivor Noel. *The Virginia Adventure: Roanoke to James Towne: An Archaeological and Historical Odyssey.* New York: Alfred A. Knopf, 1994.

Jordan IV, James M., and Frederick S. Jordan. *Virginia Beach: A Pictorial History.* n.p: Thomas F. Hale, n.d.

Kilgore, Frank, and Stacy Fowler Horton. *The Clinch River: A World Class Treasure.* St. Paul, Va.: Mountain Heritage, Inc., 2006.

Kyle, Louisa Venable. *The Witch of Pungo.* Virginia Beach, Va.: Four O'Clock Farms Publishing Co., 1973.

Lee County Historical and Genealogical Society. *Bicentennial History of Lee County Virginia 1792-1992.* Waynesville, N.C.: Don Mills, Inc., 1992.

Lofaro, Michael A. *Daniel Boone: An American Life.* Lexington, Ky.: The University Press of Kentucky, 2003.

Loth, Calder, ed. *The Virginia Landmarks Register.* Charlottesville, Va.: University Press of Virginia, 1999.

Loving, Robert. *Double Destiny.* Bristol, Tenn.: The King Printing Co., 1955.

MacArthur, Douglas. *Reminiscences.* New York: McGraw-Hill Book Company, 1964.

Mansfield, Stephen S. *Princess Anne County and Virginia Beach: A Pictorial History.* Norfolk, Va.: The Donning Company, 1989.

Mapp, Alf J., and Ramona H. *Portsmouth: A Pictorial History.* Norfolk, Va.: The Donning Company, 1989.

Mayer, Henry. *A Son of Thunder: Patrick Henry and the American Republic.* New York: Franklin Watts, 1986.

McDonald, Jr., Travis C. *Emporia: A Centennial Retrospective 1887-1987.* Lawrenceville, Va.: Brunswick Publishing Co., 1987.

McGuinn, Doug. *The "Virginia Creeper": Remembering the Virginia-Carolina Railway.* Boone, N.C.: Bamboo Books, 1998.

McKnight, Brian D. *Contested Borderland: The Civil War in Appalachian Kentucky and Virginia.* Lexington, Ky.: The University Press of Kentucky, 2006.

Meade, Robert Douthat. *Patrick Henry: Patriot in the Making.* New York: J. B. Lippincott Co., 1957.

_____. *Patrick Henry: Practical Revolutionary.* New York: J. B. Lippincott Co., 1969.

Nanney, Jr., Frank L. *South Hill, Virginia: A Chronicle of the First 100 Years.* South Hill, Va.: by the author, 2001.

Neale, Gay. *Brunswick County, Virginia: 1720-1975.* Brunswick County, Va.: Brunswick County Bicentennial Committee, 1975.

1908 Courthouse Foundation. *Bicentennial Heritage Grayson County Virginia, 1793.* Independence, Va.: 1908 Courthouse Foundation, 1995.

Patrick County Historical Society. *History of Patrick County, Virginia.* Stuart, Va.: Patrick County Historical Society, 1999.

Perret, Geoffrey. *Old Soldiers Never Die: The Life of Douglas MacArthur.* New York: Random House, Inc., 1996.

Pritchard, Emily A., and J. Rodney Lewis. *The Life and Times of the Boyd Tavern.* Boydton, Va.: The Boyd Tavern Foundation, 1998.

Reynolds, A. D. *Recollections of Major A. D. Reynolds 1847-1925.* Winston-Salem, N.C.: Reynolds House, Inc., 1978.

Rice, Otis K. *Frontier Kentucky.* Lexington, Ky.: The University Press of Kentucky, 1975.

Salmon, John S. *A Guidebook to Virginia's Historical Markers,* Virginia Department of Historic Resources. Charlottesville, Va.: University Press of Virginia, 1994.

Scales, Tony. *Natural Tunnel: Nature's Marvel in Stone.* Johnson City, Tenn.: The Overmountain Press, 2004.

Schoenbaum, Thomas J. *The New River Controversy.* Winston-Salem, N.C.: John F. Blair, Publisher, 1979.

Simpson, Bland. *The Great Dismal Swamp: A Carolinian's Swamp Memoir.* Chapel Hill, N.C.: The University of North Carolina Press, 1990.

Stevens, William Oliver. *An Affair of Honor: The Biography of Commodore James Barron, U.S.N.* Chesapeake, Va.: Norfolk County Historical Society, 1969.

St. John, Jeffrey, and Kathryn St. John. *Landmarks 1765-1990: A Brief History of Mecklenburg County, Virginia.* Boydton, Va.: Mecklenburg County Board of Supervisors, 1990.

Sturgill, Roy L. *Nostalgic Narratives and Historic Events of Southwest Virginia.* Bristol, Va.: by the author, 1991.

Summers, Lewis Preston. *History of Southwest Virginia 1746-1786, Washington County 1777-1870.* Johnson City, Tenn.: The Overmountain Press, 1989.

Tilley, Nannie M. *Reynolds Homestead 1814-1970.* Richmond, Va.: Robert Kline and Co., n.d.

Tucker, George Holbert. *Norfolk Highlights: 1584-1881.* Norfolk, Va.: Norfolk Historical Society, 1972.

Tucker, George H. *Tidewater Landfalls.* Norfolk, Va.: Landmark Communications, Inc., 1969.

Turner, Florence Kimberly. *Gateway to the New World: A History of Princess Anne County, Virginia 1607-1824.* Easley, S.C.: Southern Historical Press, 1984.

Virginia Beach Public Library. *The Beach: A History of Virginia Beach, Va.* Revised edition. Virginia Beach, Va.: Virginia Beach Public Library, 1996.

Wells, Dianne. *Roadside History: A Guide to Kentucky Highway Markers.* Frankfort, Ky.: The Kentucky Historical Society, 2002.

Whichard, Rogers Dey. *The History of Lower Tidewater Virginia.* New York: Lewis Historical Publishing Company, Inc., 1959.

Writers Program of the Works Progress Administration. *Virginia: A Guide to the Old Dominion.* New York: Oxford University Press, 1940.

Yarsinke, Amy Waters. *Virginia Beach: A History of Virginia's Golden Shore.* Charleston, S.C.: Arcadia Publishing, 2002.

Zehmer, John G., ed. *Two Mecklenburg Towns: Architectural and Historical Surveys of Boydton and Clarksville.* Richmond, Va.: Virginia Department of Historic Resources, 2003.

Articles in Journals, Magazines, and Newspapers

Bonko, Larry. "WNOR Admonished by Federal Agency Over April Fools' Day Hoax." *The Virginian-Pilot*. 5 December 1992.

Brown, Jamie. "International Paper Makes Commitment." *The Tidewater News*. 23 September 1999.

Chaltas, David, and Richard Brown. "Battle of Jonesville (The Frozen Fight)." *The Appalachian Quarterly*. March 2005.

Ernst, William. "William Barton Rogers: Antebellum Virginia Geologist." *Virginia Cavalcade*. Summer 1974.

Gilliam, Gerald T. "Crossing at Clarksville." *The Southsider*, Volume IV, Number 2. Spring 1985.

Hairston, Douglas. "A Century of Charm." *Martinsville Bulletin*. 25 May 2003.

Harrison, M. Clifford. "Murder in the Courtroom: Sensational Newspaper Accounts Distorted the Hillsville Massacre." *Virginia Cavalcade*. Summer 1967.

Hunter, Elizabeth. "The Mabrys of Mabry Mill." *Blue Ridge Country*. July 2004.

"John H. Kerr Dam 50th Anniversary Edition." *The News-Progress*. 25 September 2002.

King, Jan, and Liz Wissbaum. "Pony Roundup on Mount Rogers." *Bristol Herald Courier*. 6 May 1976.

Lindeman, Edith. "Porterfield Visits City to Complete Plans for Opening Abingdon's Barter Theatre." *Richmond Times-Dispatch*. 17 April 1946.

Lohmann, Bill. "Fiddlin' Around: Their Old-Time Mountain Music Creates a Joyful Noise, a Common Tune to Share." *Richmond Times-Dispatch*. 25 August 2002.

_____. "Home Cookin': They've Gotten Themselves into a Fine Stew in Brunswick." *Richmond Times-Dispatch*. 7 November 2004.

Messina, Debbie. "WNOR Hoax Isn't Funny to Everyone." *The Virginian-Pilot*. 2 April 1992.

Miller, Kevin. "Who'll Stop the Drain?" *The Roanoke Times*. 2 June 2002.

Nelms, Willie. "A Divided City: Bristol's Border Disputes and the Water Works War of 1889." *Virginia Cavalcade*. Spring 1979.

Price, Charles Edwin. "Death in the Afternoon." *Blue Ridge Country*. May 1998.

Roberts, Dan. "Leader Saw Swamp's Potential." *The Virginian-Pilot*. 23 July 2006.

Robertson, W. Glenn. "The Siege of Suffolk, 1863: Another Name for Futility?" *Virginia Cavalcade*. Spring 1978.

Schuster, Hendrika. "Roosevelts in Southwest Virginia." *The Historical Society of Washington County, Va. Bulletin*, Series II, No. 35, 1998.

Stolzenburg, William. "The Mussels' Message." *Nature Conservancy*. November/December 1992.

Stone, Steve. "WNOR's Morning Team Is Suspended." *The Virginian-Pilot*. 4 April 1992.

Sturgill, Mack. "First Lady Visits Whitetop." *Smyth County News & Messenger*. 18 August 1993.

Tarter, Brent. "'An Infant Borough Entirely Supported by Commerce': The Great Fire of 1776 and the Rebuilding of Norfolk." *Virginia Cavalcade*. Fall 1978.

Tennis, Joe. "Carter Fold Fans 'Cash'-In When Johnny, June Take Stage." *Bristol Herald Courier*. 16 March 1995.

_____. "Mudslinging at Its Best." *Bristol Herald Courier*. 22 April 2004.

_____. "Nearly Half-Century Later, Hank Williams' Final Journey Through Appalachian Mountains Still Poses Mystery, Conflicting Accounts." *Bristol Herald Courier*. 26 December 1999.

Troubetzkoy, Ulrich. "From Sophocles to Arthur Miller: The Barter Theatre of Virginia." *Virginia Cavalcade*. Summer 1960.

Tuck, Faye Royster. "Berry Hill." *Virginia Cavalcade*. Spring 1985.

Tucker, George H. "Butler Ruled With Iron Hand and Silver Pocket." *Norfolk Virginian-Pilot*. 30 October 1949.

Turner, Susan McNeil. "The Skipwiths of Prestwould Plantation." *Virginia Cavalcade*. Summer 1960.

Wagner, Lon. "Locals Liked the 'Chinese Corner' Label." *The Virginian-Pilot*. 22 July 1999.

Walker, Wendy. "Coffins Float From Gravesites." *The Tidewater News*. 26 September 1999.

Watkins, Raymond W. "The Hicksford Raid." *The Greensville County Historical Society*, Publication Series 1, No. 1. April 1978.

Wilson, Goodridge. "When a Roosevelt Found Health in Virginia Hills." *Richmond Times-Dispatch*. 24 February 1935.

Online Sources

Cook, Kenneth H. "Originally Built in 1770: Part of Berry Hill was 200 Years Old This Year." www.oldhalifax.com/county/berry6.htm (accessed 26 August 2006).

Rayner, Bob. "Dixon Family Determined to Bring The Cavalier on the Hill Back to Life." *Richmond Times-Dispatch*. www.hotel-online.com/News/PR2002_3rd/Jul02_TheCavalier.html (accessed 26 August 2006).

Southwest Virginia Crossroads by Joe Tennis

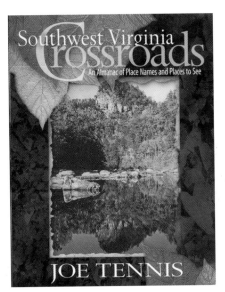

The mountains, rivers, and lakes of Southwest Virginia have invited explorers since the mid-1700s. Now this land beckons the modern traveler with its siren song of beauty, wonder, and history. *Southwest Virginia Crossroads: An Almanac of Place Names and Places to See* extols the virtues of this national treasure and serves as a guide for those who want to find the best of America.

As you journey with author Joe Tennis through *Southwest Virginia Crossroads,* he relates the history of the land and its people, chronicling the fascinating stories birthed in this fabled region, as well as age-old place-names and their origins. County maps and detailed directions lead you to all the little- and best-known attractions housed in cities and towns like Blacksburg and Abingdon or sheltered within the rolling farm-land and weathered mountains. Even those familiar with the area will want to visit waterfalls, lakes, towns, parks, fishing spots, and historical sites discovered in the pages of this comprehensive work. Whether on the car dashboard or at home on the coffee table, *Southwest Virginia Crossroads* is a wealth of knowledge and a delight to read.

ISBN: 1-57072-256-0 / $29.95 / Trade Paper

Natural Tunnel by Tony Scales

Hidden in the mountainous folds of Southwest Virginia, Natural Tunnel awaits the amazement of both seasoned acquaintances and new visitors alike. The main attraction at the 850-acre Natural Tunnel State Park, Natural Tunnel pierces Purchase Ridge for 850 feet at an average height of 50 feet and houses both a creek and a railroad—that's right, trains run through the Tunnel on a regular basis, their horns echoing off the magnificent 300-foot cliffs surrounding the Tunnel. In *Natural Tunnel: Nature's Marvel in Stone,* author and geologist Tony Scales recounts the history of the great feature, from its geologic beginnings to the first written accounts of man's interaction with the Tunnel, through a period of commercial exploitation, to the present-day state park. Richly illustrated with numerous historic photographs and geologic diagrams, *Natural Tunnel* is a must for the railfan, the casual visitor, or the die-hard fan of the treasure that is Natural Tunnel.

ISBN: 1-57072-287-0 / $19.95 / Trade Paper

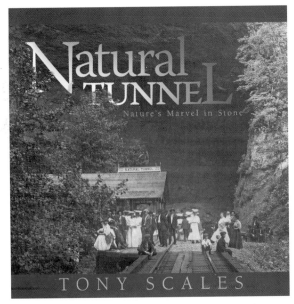